Time to Rise & Shine

A Call for the Bride of Christ to Emerge

Janice Riley

Ekklesia Arising

Published by Ekklesia Arising.

Center Point, TX 78010

ekklesiaarising.co

Paperback ISBN: 978-1-959290-02-5

eBook ISBN: 978-1-959290-03-2

For my husband, the one who patiently stood fast as I spent months working on this manuscript, encouraging, empowering and even helping me to "get my mind right" throughout this process. Thank you. This wouldn't have happened without your grace and patience being extended time and time again.

For my parents who encouraged me to read from the time I was knee-high to a grasshopper and taught me I could do anything I put my mind to. I did it!

For the OH tribe, an online community who continually challenge, communicate and support each other with love and commitment to excellence. Thank you for lifting me up to higher places in Him.

Most of all, for my Lord and Savior, the One who has been there from the beginning and will be there always. May this reach to the ends of the earth and bring You glory wherever it goes, impacting lives for good.

May God grant us grace and courage to leave behind the fetters of legalism or license and to soar as the golden eagles He has made us. Swept along in the currents of His spirit to the glorious adventure of supernatural living, attaining a joy that the shallow earthly imitation called "happiness" can never touch.

Dwight Edwards, *Revolution Within*

Contents

Introduction

Years ago, I had a vision of a herd of wild horses frolicking in a field. A mixture of breeds from all across the world, Arabians, thoroughbreds, quarter horses, Friesians, Appaloosa, even ponies mixing and mingling with the racing breeds. Each one has its own skills and talents based on its original design. Certain breeds are meant for speed. Some are skilled at amazing performances, attuned to their master. Others are bred for strength and endurance, workhorses for the harvest. Some are warhorses, specifically bred to carry His dread champions into battle. Each had been trained and groomed for a purpose: to glorify the King.

They play with outrageous joy, leaping and nipping at each other's sides in fun, chasing each other around the field. They run with wild abandon. There is no jealousy, no anger, no worry, no fear. Only love, joy, peace. Only goodness.

I believe this vision is a snapshot of what the Body of Christ is to look like in maturity and abundance. To arrive at a place where we know who we are and Whose we are, with no need to compare or compete anymore. Having released the trappings of the world that command us to strive, do more and try harder, we step into the grace and goodness of God to emerge as the beautiful butterfly He always knew we could be.

So, take a seat, buckle up and settle in for story time.

Side note: Put a pot of coffee on or start a spot of tea. Grab some cookies, along with a notepad and pen, or highlighter with little post-it tabs so you can mark up the book however you want. It's how I digest and distill books for my own studies.

Prologue

All of heaven waits on bated breath. A quiet hush has fallen over the great crowd of witnesses. Every head turned, watching and waiting. The true sleeping beauty, the hidden fairy-tale princess, lies in her bed, unconscious of the supernatural truth of her identity. The lovely one is in an identity crisis. The evil one has stolen her true spiritual identity. She stumbles through each day, miserable and broken, depressed and oppressed. Blind and deaf to the truth. Called to reign with Jesus, the Bride wanders the earth with amnesia, clueless to who she really is.

She hears the voice of the enemy: tirades, curses, taunts, tormenting thoughts, endless bullying, nagging snipes of incompetence, insecurity and unimportance. The onslaught of negativity never ceases. She stumbles. She crumbles into her bed, burnt out and worn out. Sick and tired of being sick and tired. She thinks, *There has to be more to this life. This can't be all there is.*

A horn sounds, its echo pierces through the thickest walls. Everyone knows the time has come. It is time for the beauty to awaken. Heaven breathes deeply as they watch the Lover charge across the sky on His white steed. A cheer erupts from one end to the other as they admire the bravery and confidence of their King. Brilliant Light surrounds Him as He soars through the clouds.

The enemy's minions try to stop Him, they attempt to hinder His flight to His beloved's side. Far excelling any Chuck Norris or Jackie Chan move, the Lover fights tooth and nail through the hordes of hell, the raging wickedness of his ancient enemies. With a slash to the left, a sword swing to the right and the occasional battle cry that shakes the mountains, He steadily makes His way through the battle zone to His beloved.

He enters her home, rushes to her bedside. He leans over and gently kisses her lips. “Arise, My Lovely One, arise. Your time has come. It is time to come forth and be honored as My Bride. It is time for Our Wedding; it is time to reign.”

Chapter One

A Voice Crying Out

There is a voice crying out in the wilderness, in the city streets, in the desolate wastelands, in the depths of the harshest prisons, amid secret brothels, inside large office towers and city halls. A voice crying out for the lost children of the Living God to come alive. Just as a lighthouse shines a beam to guide the ships at sea, these voices serve as beacons calling the missing ones home.

Amid darkness, poverty, shame, fear, despair, hopelessness, there is a Voice saying, "I am here. I am near. You have endured enough. I don't care what you've done. It doesn't matter. You are Mine. I am the One who created you. You are Mine. It's time to come learn who you really are. Learn to live in the fullness of your identity."

Can you hear the voice? Can you hear the call to come alive? Have you felt the shift from brokenness to wholeness? Have you felt the urge to transform into something, someone new? To emerge from the chrysalis and see what happened during your time in the quiet and stillness of surrender? If so, you're in for a delightful ride.

Ponder this.

Have you considered how focused we are on the cross? You see it everywhere. Many people wear it on a necklace or other jewelry, it is on our clothing, our bibles, it's everywhere. The whole church celebrates Resurrection Sunday every year, some with a focus on Holy Week, an intentional look at the final days of Jesus' life, from Palm Sunday to

Easter Sunday. Reliving the passion of Christ, the sacrifice, the pain He endured for us.

The Church has been focused on proclaiming Her Bridegroom has risen; He is alive. Yes, a worthy Lamb was slain to pay the ultimate price, a willing sacrifice, for the children of God. The crucifixion of one man changed the world forever. A man who then rose from the grave three days later with the keys to death, hell and the grave.

We celebrate the day Jesus rose from the grave. We dance because He lives. We hoop and holler because He did not stay in the tomb. We shout because He is alive.

Yet, Heaven watches the Body of Christ these days, sitting on the edge of their seats, if you will. The great crowd of witnesses might even stand to their feet, just to observe our every move, hang on our every word. You see, Heaven knows what's coming. Heaven is focused on the coming Kingdom of God, the new Jerusalem. A new age is dawning. The days foretold by the great prophets of Scripture are about to take place. So much is being orchestrated behind the scenes. Things are falling into place; the wedding day is approaching.

Heaven waits in eager anticipation for the Church to realize who She really is ... the Bride of Christ. For her to rule and reign with the King, to live as royalty, to walk with boldness and courage as she advances the Kingdom of God.

It is time for the Church to arise from the grave, to stop wandering the earth as hopeless orphans and walk, to run with wings as eagles, to fully embrace who she is in Christ. To know she is redeemed, renewed and refreshed. Will you live life on this earth as liberated warrior, letting go of the past, releasing everything that's not of God, uprooting all the things that hinder, to kill flesh once and for all?

It is time to walk into family dinners, schools, offices, factories, hospitals, city halls, the capitol with the authority and power His resurrection has given us.

It is time to step out of the boat known as religion and fly out of the cage known as trauma and fear. It is time to discover who we really are in Christ, to fulfill the Great Commission and discover what happens when we transform into His likeness.

We are being shaped for His purpose. We are being refined by the fire. Think of Daniel in the lion's den. Think of Shadrach, Meshach and Abednego in the fiery furnace. Think of Paul and Silas, imprisoned and yet continuing to praise His holy name. What did their faith during their trials accomplish? They endured through the storms of life and saw the supernatural manifest before their very eyes because of their faith in the one true God.

Now we are the ones being called into and prepared for His service. We are the ones in the middle of the fire, held captive in prison, enduring trials while the world and heaven looks on, watching to see if we will growl, grumble and groan or will we renew our faith and praise Him during the circumstance.

The time has come for us to unite as the Body of Christ, to walk this earth in the boldness, courage and grace of who we really are. To live a life worth living, one that honors those who went before us.

We need to get a purpose, a plan. We need to approach this with some serious offensive behavior. No more letting the weasels of the world run your life, letting them walk over you. Have you had enough? Are you ready to claim what is rightfully yours, put on your boxing gloves and enter the ring?

I can tell you I am sick and tired of seeing others as well as myself be attacked every minute of every day. I am tired of the worry and strife. I am tired of seeing godly people being struck down by the evil one and I'm tired of seeing churches ripped apart because they let the evil one enter her doors. I am not going to take it anymore.

Are you ready to join me in learning how to walk like Christ, to shine with His glory?

Take a trip with me as I wander through years of morning journals with the Lord, worship journals and "Papa, what is on Your heart today?" moments of my life. I have compiled these prayers, these sweet whispers of hope and joy, these invigorating charges from the Holy Spirit into a book that makes sense (or so I hope) and has some hands-on activations and activities for you to implement.

We are being called to live a life worthy of His sacrifice and love. He's asking us to step up to the plate, bat in hand, and knock it out of the park. Jesus is calling us to embrace our identity in Him and truly live it day by day until we get to see Him face to face for eternity.

But first, let's find our way to home plate, to our starting point, and assess the situation.

Chapter Two

Just Breathe

When you look around, it looks as if a bomb went off. It feels like you're being attacked on all sides. Every aspect of your life is under fire, and you are searching for a place to hide for a moment of rest, a simple place of refuge. When you think you can't handle one more thing, something else happens. Another one of the many plates you had spinning in the air crashes to the floor.

You cringe at the sound of the crash and cry out, "Lord, I can't take any more. I thought You loved me. I thought You were going to bless me, prosper me. What is this? It sure doesn't look like blessings and favor to me. What are You doing? What did I do wrong? I said I'd follow you anywhere. I said I was all in. I said I am Yours. I don't understand. I don't get this. I don't get You."

And you collapse in a heap to the ground.

Beloved, do you sense the Father drawing close to you, His much-loved child? He hears your every cry. He strokes your head, kisses your brow.

Beloved, My dear heart, breathe. Breathe in My Peace. Just breathe. You are focused on what's wrong according to your current mindset rather than focusing on Me. You are magnifying the trials, injuries, offenses, the drama in your life rather than magnifying My Holy Name. In order to get you to where I have called you, I need to develop your character, your endurance, your perseverance. Removing every fire, every trial from your life, would prevent you from being refined by MY FIRE. *This is molding you into a beautiful vessel I can use for My glory. Just as the gardener uproots weeds, trims the trees, prunes off dead branches, I am trimming you to shape you into a gorgeous, fruit-bearing tree. I desire to bring forth more fruit in your life.*

I am working on you, dear child, to mold you into the likeness of My Son, Jesus Christ. I am changing you into My bold and courageous warrior. You must learn to abide in Me, to focus on Me alone. When doubts, fears, worries seep into your mind, immediately take them captive. Identify who is sponsoring those thoughts. If it's not a thought from heaven, get rid of it. Replace it with a thought from heaven. This is the first battle you must win. Before you take territory for the Kingdom, you need to take the battlefield of your mind.

If you are like me, after hearing that, your response is, "Let's do this. I am with you, Lord."

Let me tell you. It's gonna get messy. Things may even break. Tears will fall. Blood will be shed. Veils will be torn. Lamentations and shouts of praise will be cried. The damaged, hurt, broken, traumatized pieces of your heart and soul will find safety, a place of security, a haven where they can be seen and finally know they are accepted, loved and healed.

Find that five-point safety harness your mother wanted you to wear when you started driving and strap in. The ride has begun.

He is doing something new on the earth. The Lord is bringing forth something new in us. Many of us have been carrying new ministries, businesses, books, endeavors, adventures, for years now. The Lord is saying it's time for a baby boom across the land. We need to realize birthing something new requires time, commitment, persistence, endurance, dying to self, accepting what God is doing in you and through you. Surrendering to His plan and purpose in this new season. Letting go of what you thought was good. Releasing your hold on all things, all people, all places, letting go of everything but Jesus.

OK, Janice, you think, *I hear you but really? Seriously? Does it really require ALL that?*

Yes, beloved, it does. I'll share more of my story as we progress through this book. For now, I'll simply say I went from living in Maryland where I managed a technical innovation center, working with tech startups, small business, and economic development to abiding in Hill Country, Texas, running a business out of my home with a focus on all things publishing. I went from putting a smile on my face and ignoring the pile of moldy, crusty, stinky dung that was under the rug to a serene, peace-filled, confident woman who knows her identity in Christ and knows who her Father is. A woman who had pulled up the rug and swept up all the dirt, dead mice and crumbs of food that had been shoved under there for decades.

I asked for more of God. I asked to be used by God. I put myself on the altar, saying, "Here I am. Use me." I sang songs for years, asking Him to make me a servant, to break my heart for what breaks His. I even told Him to tear down strongholds. Anything I had erected in my heart, my soul, my life that didn't serve Him, wasn't of Him, I wanted it destroyed.

Then He answered those prayers. Yeshua pulled back the layers one by one, revealing heartache, trauma, the roots of fear of abandonment, rejection, betrayal. He gently opened up the wounds that had never truly healed fully, pouring His Living Water upon me as He conducted surgery upon my heart. He applied the healing balm of Gilead to each place He worked, giving me time to process and heal before beginning work on the next place on His list. It has been a journey of healing and deliverance.

Amid my journey through the wilderness, in the dark night of soul, during chaos and confusion, Jesus was there. In the pain, the trauma, in the fire's intensity, Jesus was next to me. Yes, there were moments I couldn't feel His presence. There were times I couldn't see or hear Him. A season of hiddenness gave me the opportunity to discover His presence is not dependent on my ability to sense His nearness. He was with me, Immanuel, even if I didn't feel His Presence.

He whispers,

Fix your eyes on Me. Though the storm rages, the winds roar, the waves crash in, the rain torrents down, stay in My Presence. Stay focused on Me. Block out the lies, fears, doubts trying to creep in. Choose to abide in

My Presence. Breathe out frustration, anxiety, fear, worry, and irritation. Breathe in life, blessing, peace, joy, and love. The enemy wants to steal your peace, your joy, your faith. His tactics are focused on those things. Realize what his agenda is; use your shield and sword accordingly.

Chapter Three

He Sings Over Us

The Lord your God in your midst, the Mighty One, will save; He will rejoice over you with gladness, He will quiet you with His love, He will rejoice over you with singing.

Zephaniah 3:17 NKJV

He sings over us. What song is He singing over you? What is its theme, its message? What is its melody? Who is singing harmony? What instruments accompany His voice?

There is a message in His song over you. There is a banner held high. He calls forth your identity. Awakening seeds of destiny. Declaring freedom and liberty over you. Bringing peace and joy to every nook and cranny of your heart, your soul. He anoints your head with oil. It runs down over your shoulders, your body.

He calls you His child. He sees you as lovely, treasured, holy and redeemed.

He has chosen you to be His child, His son or daughter.

Listen to the Father's whispers of Shalom for you.

Breathe in My peace. Open the door to your well-guarded heart and let the King of Glory in. Breathe again. Let the oxygen fill your lungs as your chest expands. Let all of your worries, cares, concerns fall to the ground as you breathe in My peace. Feel My love surrounding you. Let it soak into every part of you. My glory is all around you. Seeping into every skin cell, penetrating your walls. My light pierces the darkness, causing it to flee.

Ask Me to shine in you, and through you to eradicate the darkness. Ask me to intervene, to engage.

Rest is a weapon. We use this weapon by being still and knowing He is God, by pushing away negative thoughts and stressful feelings. Learning to ABIDE in His Presence. Soak in His Love.

Joyful Christians get more opportunities. Speak gracious and attractive words and you'll be a magnet to new endeavors and projects. We have to be the Light to those seeking the light.

Training for Gaining

How much do you want to grow, to develop, to mature?

I mean, really. Take a seat and be real for a minute. Don't give me the good little Christian answer. Don't feed me a line of cow manure. I can smell it a mile away. Don't tell me what your mind thinks is the right answer. You've done that way too many times already.

Take a deep breath. Inhale for a count of four. Release it. Do it again. And again. OK, now you're ready. Allow me to ask again. How much do you want to be transformed into the likeness of Christ?

I can see the confused look in your eyes, so let me explain why I am asking so pointedly. It is time to dig in your heels and stand regardless of what things look like. Your flesh, your bitter root judgments, your belief systems, your religion are all about to crumble into a heap.

1. Your flesh needs to die so you can walk surrendered to His call. Not hesitating because you might look weird or wonder what someone might think. Not offended because someone looked at you funny or you didn't get a prophetic word from the guy on stage.

2. Those bitter root judgments are now expectations that affect your life on so many levels. Judge not lest you be judged. Do you realize the bitterness you're harboring is harming you and others? That stance saying every leader, supervisor is going to take advantage of you, take credit for your work, overlook you for promotion, ridicule you... causes those very things to happen. Isn't it time to change?

3. Your subconscious has beliefs contrary to what your good Christian mind thinks. Contrary to what Scripture says. Rewiring, revising, reworking these systems are possible; it simply requires focus and effort. The belief that you won't ever amount to anything, that your business will never truly succeed, rooted back to childhood days where your uncle told you this regularly, has to be identified and broken. It needs to be replaced with a Scripture-based truth.

4. Your religion. Click. Click. Boom. The Godhead wants a relationship with you, not a religion filled with performance and rituals. You can walk through the motions of a worship service and never even encounter Him. Your assumptions that you have to be good, serve, give, in order to be loved by God are religion based and not of Jesus. Who told you that?

I could go on, but I believe we have an excellent base here, enough that you are grasping how much excavation is about to happen in your mind, heart, and soul. A bit of advice: grab a pick and an ax. Those rocks of self-righteousness need to be busted up as well.

Are you committed enough to risk failure? Willing to overcome your fear of looking weird, silly, or strange? Ready to give up that desire to impress someone you think is a VIP?

If you want to climb higher on the glory mountain, you must be ready, willing and able to train. To unload anything in your backpack that adds unnecessary weight. The journey will make you feel every extra ounce in your pack that's not needed for what's ahead.

As we start the journey of digging, earth moving, to prepare the ground for a foundation to be laid, the building to be constructed, we discover childish ways, fleshly habits that need to be dug up. Jesus said, "You have heard it said, but now I say...." Teaching us to use a Kingdom language, not one of world and flesh. He was the originator of the opposite tactic, the "have another thought" challenge Graham Cooke issues regularly.

Let's review a few fears plaguing the Body of Christ these days. Which ones do you battle? (Notice I didn't write "have" there. Word choice is important. Stop claiming the fears, the diseases, the problems, and start declaring the fight is on!)

1. Fear of failure

2. Fear of being found out as imposter

3. Fear of loss

4. Fear of death

5. Fear of success

6. Fear of rejection

Fear is the delivery system of the enemy. You end up trapped in misunderstandings. You fear what could go wrong and find yourself delivered to a place where you act out of fear. Your mind storyboards scenarios of defeat instead of walking from victory.

Stop borrowing from negative possibilities and fix your eyes on Jesus.

Training for gaining starts with Love. Maybe you can recite 1 Corinthians 13 to me right now. That means you have hidden the passage in your mind. King David said he hid the Word of the Lord in his *heart*. What's the difference between hiding something in your mind and in your heart? Glad you asked.

Let me explain. You could say you *know* that biblical passage. You know it well enough to recite it. That means you've memorized the words to the point you can regurgitate it on command. But let's dig deeper on the word know. Just as we can dive into scripture utilizing the Strong's Concordance and analyzing the Hebrew/Greek root words of the passage, we can deliberate on the verb *know.* There are many meanings of the word know. Adam *knew* Eve in Genesis and they conceived Seth. There's an intimacy there, an experiential knowledge. I know how to bake a cake. I also know my husband loves me. There is a drastic difference between those two usages of the verb know. My husband has told me of his love and shown me this to be true many times over the last twenty-plus years. It's an experiential kind of knowledge.

Our belief systems, our subconscious, are based on what we've hidden in our hearts. If our subconscious believes all supervisors will steal our ideas and claim them as their own, they'll treat us like redheaded stepchildren, we'll live a life expecting that behavior to manifest. If we believe despite our best efforts, nothing will change, we'll never get ahead, guess what will happen. If our childhood trauma taught us that people aren't to be trusted, they will eventually abandon and/or betray you, we'll have trust issues with anyone and everyone. We'll have self-protection walls in place to keep ourselves safe. Then we wonder why we don't have close friends.

Ask Jesus to shine His light on whatever strongholds you have, whatever false belief systems are in place. Ask Him to illuminate what lies you've been believing about Him, yourself or others. Seek the wisdom to go with these revelations to enable you to process these things with the Holy Spirit.

My friend, Alison Bown, once said, "Every lie of the devil is meant to reduce you, confine you and eliminate you. Don't cooperate with that process." Our goal now is to identify which lies we're still believing, which ones are holding us captive and come out of agreement with them, renounce them.

This may seem like work. This may seem like advanced training in the military. Haven't you realized you're in His army and we go through various types of training regularly? That being said, shouldn't we be passionate about the training instead of complacent or dreading it? Shouldn't we shift into the gear of being still, listening and responding to the Father amid the mess? Too often we remain in the gear of anxiety, fear, chaos, and confusion. It's time we learned to shift higher, shift into a place of peace, serenity and calmness. We should learn to welcome the opportunity to grow and transform into the likeness of Christ, rather than wallow in the pit with the pigs.

When we know, really know, we are His children, sons and daughters of the Most High King, we have a mindset shift. We take on a majestic mindset. We replace a slave mindset with not just a son's mindset, but a royal son, a prince.

We accept Jesus as Lord and Savior. We get water baptized and declare the old man is gone and new has come. Then the time comes to walk out that declaration. When an unexpected bill comes, do we curse our finances and rant about how we can never get ahead? Or do we thank the Father, Jehovah Jireh for being our provider and trusting Him to come through, delivering whatever we need in the moment? Standing on His promises, determining you cannot fail with the Lord on your side.

Chapter Four

Bitter Root Judgments

Let's deal with those bitter roots I previously mentioned.

"Bitter Roots?" you ask. "Wait, I'm not a tree, I'm a person. What do you mean, I have bitter roots to deal with?" Well, we are challenged to be oaks of righteousness in Psalms, aren't we? When Jesus healed a blind man, he first saw men as trees walking around and then Jesus touched him again. But I digress.

We develop bitter root judgments based on life because of what's happened in our past. When one pastor rejects, mistreats us, we then judge him, calling him names and choose to erect a wall between us. We then judge other pastors the same way and expect them to behave accordingly. Just like a jealous boyfriend whose first girlfriend cheated on him, and so he berates and accuses each girl thereafter of doing the same thing. He actually pushes them into said behavior because he curses them with it so often.

Let's dive into a more personal example. Years ago, I was working with several female bosses fifteen to twenty years older than I was. After the first two tried to sabotage my career there, I developed a knee-jerk reaction to older women. I didn't trust them and unconsciously expected them to behave as the first ones did. The CEO brought on more management, same gender, same age.

I'm sure you aren't surprised to know the second verse was the same as the first. Only this one took it up a notch. They once invited me to lunch with the two of them, only to tell me how they would fire me if they had the power and continued to berate me. Things got worse instead of better.

I finally went to the boss and told him, "If you hire one more woman over the age of fifty, I am going to smack you alongside the head." Admittedly, I was a spitfire and my mouth/attitude wasn't fully saved yet. I had asked Jesus into my heart, but we were still deliberating and negotiating my mouth at the time. Maybe that's why I used to have recurring dreams about wearing a mouth retainer. He was telling me He was putting restrictions and molds on my mouth to maintain a straight design. Anyhow, back to the story. Thankfully, my CEO and I had worked together enough. He took it all in stride and simply laughed at my feistiness.

Nowadays, I can recognize the soul wounds I was bearing in those days. I see the bitter roots that had grown into full trees by that time of my life. I have spent years working with the Holy Spirit to peel back the layers of my heart and uproot the weeds of discord, distrust, accusation, betrayal, abandonment, and whatever else not of Him.

I realize my stance and expectations contributed to why certain things happened the way they did. My unresolved issues provided an open door for strife and discord. Therefore, it is so important to eradicate anything in us that is not of Him. It's time to empty yourself.

Empty Yourself.

Empty yourself of all the lies, the confusion.

Every piece of apathy, every smidgen of indifference, every tiny fraction of the feeling *you're not good enough, you're not pretty, you're stupid* needs to go.

Remove every piece of mistaken identity, of confusion, of laziness, of status quo, of incompetence, of worry, fear, discord, concern. Every piece needs to go.

Grab every bit and byte of hate, self-rejection, self-loathing. Rip it off and throw it away.

Walk through your soul house. Examine every room, closet, every cubbyhole, nook and cranny. No secret places left. No hiding spots exist anymore. Cleanse the entire house.

I am coming with an all-consuming fire. I am igniting it from the ground level, from your very foundation and I'm setting YOU on fire. Anything not of Me is gone, vanished in flames of Glory. Every hindrance, everything that bound you to your past is gone. Completely engulfed, consumed. There is nothing left but what I bring forth from the ashes, beauty from ashes. I bring strength from fear, gladness for mourning, and peace for despair.

Prepare yourself for the fire by taking every weed, every root, everything I told you to remove from its improper place in you and throwing it onto the altar of My temple, your body. Get ready for Me to burn up the sacrifices.

My fire heals. My fire renews. My fire revives the dead. My fire redeems the lost. Feel the fire as I set it deep in your bones, so deep, it cannot be put out.

Chapter Five

Take the Leap

Ever take a leap of faith into the unknown? Ever felt the Lord calling you to start a new business, move to a different state, or go to a foreign land to serve Him? Your risk might have been being let go of one job unexpectedly and having to rely on the Lord to provide for your needs, to provide a new job or the inkling needed to launch your own company. Whatever the type of risk, I'm sure you've been prompted to take at least one.

What if entering new territories, new lands, new industries, new endeavors isn't as risky as the spirit of fear would like us to think? What if a mindset shift was all we needed to decimate our stress levels and improve our physical health within days? What if we learned to rejoice at higher levels in such a way, we discover how to recognize tests, to cooperate with the Lord as He leads us into the wilderness, into the promised land (depending on which season of life you're in)? With this perspective shift, we see tests, trials, and certain circumstances as opportunities to mature in Christ, to be transformed into His likeness, to advance. We see a whole new world through different lenses once we get a new prescription from Jesus.

Beloved, it is time to come into a full revelation. There are no risks with God when we keep our eyes on Him and embrace our tests because we know how to make the most of them. Positioned as more than conquerors.

Do you hear Him calling you up higher to take greater risks?

He's calling us deeper, deeper into the wells of joy.

He is calling us out to the depths of oceans of love.

He's calling us out onto the white waters of the rivers of mercy and grace.

He's calling out to the stillness of His lakes of glory.

He stands there, staring at His beloved with eyes of love and fire, waiting for Her to respond, for Her to come, to come with Him.

Will you leave the shores of safety?

Will you release the ties that bind you to the banks of the rivers?

Will you let go of what's known and follow Him into the unknown?

Will you put your hand in His and just go, content to be wherever He is.

Walk in the days numbered for you.

Be irritated with His dreams about you.

Have an itch that doesn't let you rest until you venture out beyond your comfort.

Out with Him, where you can't see the bottom, where you have no hope of touching the bottom anymore. Where ships sail and sea creatures lurk. Out with Him.

Waves come. Winds blow. Storms rage. Sharks may circle. Pirates may attack. Supplies for the journey might look sparse. Injuries may come because of the danger zone you have entered. The possibilities are endless.

One thing is sure. He is with you. He will never leave you nor forsake you. If you stay focused on Him, and not on the winds, the waves, the raging storm, the circling sharks, or the prowling pirates, you shall remain content and peaceful, abiding in Him.

As you rely on Him to provide for every need, every step of the way, you get to see supernatural provision. Miracles happen as He moves mountains on your behalf. You will only experience the adventure, the excitement, the joy, the delight of this journey, if you go!

Will you say "yes"?

Chapter Six

The Unmasked Face

Many of us have hidden secrets and infected soul wounds behind pretty smiles and theater masks we've worn inside the church for too long. What if we choose to live life as an open book instead? Being vulnerable and transparent with the truth, the reality of our situations? James knew something about this.

Therefore, confess your sins to one another and pray for one another, that you may be healed. James 5:16a NLT

There is healing in confession. We have allowed pride and fear of man to keep us bound and scared. Too fearful of what someone might think if she really knew the truth about how imperfect we really are. Or we don't want to lose cool points by being transparent about what we're going through, the oppression that won't lift off of us, the rebellious child we're dealing with, the marital discord we're enduring. Solomon said in Lamentations, there is nothing new under the sun. Do you really think you're the only one battling X, dealing with Y and just avoiding Z? When we seize a moment of bravery and bare our souls, when we explain the drama and trauma we're going through, we fight off the enemy's weapons of isolation, rejection and abandonment. We let down our walls and let others in so they can support, encourage, and empower us. We were created to be connected.

> There is a release and a healing that flows from confessing not only to God in the secret place of your heart but also to a trusted friend, or to the person you have offended. The tender words, "I'm sorry, will you forgive me?" are one of the surest paths to joy. John Piper, *When the Darkness Will Not Lift*

Don't you know God opposes the proud but gives grace to the humble? Pride equals arrogance. Humility comes with transparency and authenticity. We need more of both in the world today.

Beloved, it's time to see yourself clean. Innocent. Pure. Humble. Simple. Regardless of what you've been through, the trauma endured, Jesus' blood redeems you and makes you new. You are now clothed in robes of righteousness.

Surround yourself with others walking in holiness and righteousness. Have relationships with others who exude those qualities.

Be in a relationship with your Lord. Simple prayers uttered to the Father from a much-loved child are exactly what He wants to hear from your lips. Ask the Lord what you should ask for. What is God's will for your life?

Let's go back to pride for a moment. Its mask means you never ask the simple questions. It prevents answers; it destroys relationships. Only you can remove the mask.

How do you remove it? Fast. Humble yourself before God. Go lower.

Go lower, lower still, My child. I will raise you up from the depths of the pit. I will set your feet on high places. I will bring you out of the fire, a fully alive, fully engaged child of Mine. A warrior champion who advances my Kingdom.

Look for ways to serve others, to step out of your box in a way that changes the atmosphere, for ways to stop focusing on yourself. Live out of your will, not your emotions. Keep your mind on God. In His Presence there is fullness of joy. And the joy of the Lord is our strength.

Speaking of Self.

Self-centeredness. Self-absorbed. Self-rejection. Self-loathing. Self-destruction. Self-harm. Self-esteem. Self-love. Self-hatred.

(Are we really *all* narcissists?)

It's not about you. Selfies. Social Media. Reality TV. This era has turned us into a navel-gazing generation, concerned about how we look and sound, expecting every hair to be in place and makeup to be perfect for every photo. There's an app for that. We even have apps to fix our faces before we post it online. Because we don't like how we look naturally. Use it to shave off those extra twenty pounds.

Yet the world cries out for authentic, raw and true. For transparency, vulnerability. When you let the walls down, you take the masks off and remove the blinders, you can finally truly love, really connect to the Father and others. We hunger for genuine community and connection; yet our walls of self preservation keep others at a safe distance so we don't get hurt.

We hear lies from the enemy: others wouldn't like us if they saw the true us, the girl underneath the mask. If we let go of our tough guy exterior, who will protect us?

We've been told we're fat, stupid, ugly, helpless, hopeless, no good, so forth and so on for decades. We're unloveable.

We've accepted those false labels as truth. Regardless of who said them, we've taken them inside our hearts and minds, our souls and based our lives upon those precepts. Then we wonder why nothing changes. Breakthrough never comes. Our subconscious keeps enforcing the walls of doubt and discord.

Then self-rejection begins. We don't like ourselves; we actually hate the person we see in the mirror. In reality, we would never talk to another human being the way we talk to ourselves. Self-loathing, self-hatred take up occupying our souls and our minds. Sickness and disease enter because of the self rejection we have.

- Lupus
- Migraines
- Autoimmune diseases
- Cancer
- Digestive ailments

Our bodies attack itself as a result, a reaction to the self-rejection and self hatred we feel. Our bodies are merely responding to our thoughts and actions. Then we wonder what's going on and what's wrong. So much of our ailments in how we view ourselves and God.

Isn't it time we surrendered all of it, all the pain and trauma? Allow me to share my story about surrendering it to Jesus.

There I stood, before Jesus, with my heart in my hand.

"Here's my heart, Lord. It's been broken, stepped on, shattered, slashed with a knife, pierced by swords, ripped in two, abused, and healed with scars. Healed imperfectly. It's a mess. I am amazed sometimes it still beats. It has been through years of heartache and disappointment, fear and confusion, anxiety and intimidation. Scared of being hurt yet again.

"But, Lord, You said You wanted it. You asked me to give it to You. So here it is. I'm surrendering it to You to do with as You will."

"My child, I want you to surrender your wounded heart so I can give you a new heart full of Me, My joy, My peace, My goodness, My love."

Integrity of the Heart

There is a battle over our hearts. Why our hearts? Indigenous tribes used to cut out the hearts of their fresh kills and eat them raw. By doing so, they believed they could receive all the qualities of the animal – bravery, strength and agility.[1]

The heart empowers the body to race, to run, to live. Our hearts pump life blood through our veins, enabling us to live. Abundant life comes by giving our hearts to the Beloved. True joy, everlasting peace, redemption and courage, a boldness that conquered Golaith as a small shepherd boy enters our bodies.

He wants to purify our hearts so our blood takes oxygen and healing to every organ, every tissue, every cell of our body. So tell me, what's in the depths of your heart? Who are you when you're by yourself? What choices do you make? Do you struggle to be alone, truly alone, and just sit before the Lord?

It is time to learn to be alone and be at peace. To be still and know He is God and He will be exalted among the nations. To quiet our hearts, minds and souls.

---

1. "Hearts in Their Mouths." Game & Fish Magazine. October 31, 2013. https://www.gameandfishmag.com/editorial/hearts-in-their-mouths/365866#:~:text=Eating%20the%20heart%20out%20of,%E2%80%93%20bravery%2C%20strength%20and%20agility.

Let Him develop the skills in you so you can reach someone through them. Make choices based on the knowledge of what He has entrusted to YOU. Be whole in Christ, not divided, not double-minded. Reflect on who the Father says you are. Be real. Be authentic. Walk out your identity in Christ.

Let nothing hide in the closet any longer, but come clean with anything that causes shame. Stop giving the enemy an open door to torment and torture you. The Father can redeem all things. Love covers a *MULTITUDE* of sin. It's time to deal with the areas of the heart where darkness has seeped in.

Find a trusted friend, a spiritual mentor near you, and schedule some time to talk. My pastor calls his inner healing and deliverance sessions, true ministry sessions, "couch sessions." If you're feeling irritable, cantankerous, out of sorts, it's probably a good time to schedule some couch time. Need help to track down someone to talk to? Track me down online and I'll talk with you personally. I'll help you find your way to peace.

Jesus stands at the door and knocks. Open the door and invite Him in. Bring Him into your wounds, hurts, secret closets and the dark, dreary basement you avoid. Let Him in with His Love and Light. Watch and see what He will do. Taste and see that the Lord is good. To refine you and renew you into His likeness.

Jesus declares,

I am going through your heart, clearing out debris, clutter, flotsam, picking up litter along the roads. I am cleaning up messes, putting things away in their proper homes, organizing what belongs there, so it all fits perfectly.

Trash, toxins, poisons, and other items not meant to be stored in your heart are being removed.

I am increasing its size to bring more inside. More Joy. More Peace. More Love. As you grasp the depths of My spiritual fruit growing inside of your heart, I now ask you to let My children in. I want you to share your heart with those to whom I have called you. I have cleansed it and refined you. Now I want you to open your heart with the nations. Stay in Me. Your security is in Me. Let My words root deep within your soul. I ask you to give more because I have more to give you.

Chapter Seven

The Process Changes You

The process of transformation, of renewal, makes you more valuable. Do you not realize gold found in the ground must go through refining, through processing before it's ready to be made into jewelry or functional? A grape is just a grape, but after processing and stomping, it becomes a wine. In the agriculture industry, "value-added" products are raw ingredients transformed into something new through a process. Yes, the process and addition of various ingredients make the good more valuable than its original state. We are the same way. As we mature into His likeness, we produce more fruit in our lives, bringing more value to the Kingdom of Heaven.

Paul Keith Davis puts it succinctly in his book *Thrones of Our Soul*.

> "It is through the stripping process and assuming the heart of a servant that true spiritual authority is recognized in heaven. A bondservant is one who yields his will to the will of his master. If we embrace the correct commission, we will be catapulted to greater measures of loving kindness, and righteousness and experience heightened expressions of His glory. Many of the events taking place in our generation will be unprecedented circumstances

> requiring counsel that will come from behind the veil through the Spirit of wisdom and revelation. We must be willing to pay the price to be cleansed and purified to be joined with Christ and taken to the Throne Room of God to receive our instruction and begin to comprehend the mysteries of the Kingdom."

Speaking of comprehending the mysteries of the Kingdom, check out this whisper of the Father.

My love, you have yet to see the tip of the iceberg, a slightest spark of My Power. Wait till you see the Glory, the Power I am releasing upon My saints, my precious ones, those who have pursued Me above all else, who have forsaken it all for the sake of My call, who have died to self. I am pouring out a fire upon them that cannot be extinguished. I am setting a fire down deep in their bones that will ignite the world. My power is being released by filing them with a greater measure of my love. As they LOVE, My power flows to them, through them and from them.

Our challenge is obedience. Submission. Denial of self. Refusal to settle for status quo. Discontent with staying the same, with being lukewarm, with average and normal. Total surrender. Relinquishing any right to self, to life outside the will of God.

It is us truly saying, "Here am I, Lord, send me," while standing on our toes, ready to run. Being willing to go wherever He sends without complaint. Obeying His commands, submitting one's will to His. So in love with Him, nothing else will do. In awe of His Glory, enamored with His Presence, to such a degree, nothing else matters.

A surrendered one follows where He leads. The bond slave answers when the Lord calls. When God asks, they give.

The Lord set apart these children of the Most High God. Chosen. Called. Sanctified. Hungry for more of heaven on earth. Thirsty for the Living Waters. They are not content to sit on the sidelines and watch. They are not willing to warm the bench while others battle for the win. These are the unique ones, the different ones, the peculiar children who just don't fit in.

Surrendered. Sacrificed. Given over to complete surrender to Christ, to *LOVE*. To walk with the Lord, to talk with the Lord, to rest in the Lord. To abide with Him. His glory shines on one's face after spending time with Him. One acts like Him, looks like Him, talks like Him, because of spending so much time with Him.

Chapter Eight

Battle-ready Weapons

I have an arsenal full of an array of weapons, from different eras, different battles, different cultures. The weapons of the medieval knight, the Japanese samurai, the Native American brave, the Spartan warrior and many others are represented in My armory. Each has a different purpose and usage in battle.

Dusty and rusty weapons, unused for decades, ones that supposed they'd seen their last day of battle are now being refired, retested, cleaned and oiled once again as I ready them for battle. These weapons have been through countless skirmishes, battles, wars over the centuries. They may be dirty, rusty, missing a few parts now, but I have a plan to use them in the coming Day of the Lord. I will redeem their service. I will renew their strength. I will restore their form, their health so they might serve Me fully.

I am retooling them for a new form of battle, supernatural war. I am reframing them into novel forms. Weapons the world has never seen before are being brought forth. I am bringing out munition specialists trained by Me in order to refit, reform, retrain, retool this arsenal, this pile of weapons for the coming battle. They have been through advanced training in My institute to learn how to do this work. They will show the masses how to praise Me in new ways, how to give thanks with every breath they take. How to walk in wisdom, how to dance with abandon upon injustice, how to abide in peace amid chaos, how to decree life and abundance into existence, how to declare righteousness and love in every situation.

There is more action, more engagement ahead for these weapons than seen in prior battles.

As barrels of guns overheat, warp and wear, they get replaced with new ones. I am releasing new missions, new mandates to each of those weapons stored inside the arsenals of the Church. These weapons were stored in closets of old buildings, unwanted and unused because others didn't see their value or understand their purpose and destiny.

There are closets full of dusty, rusty weapons all over the world. I am sending in gunsmiths to raid those closets and repair, renovate, and modify these weapons for My service. Carvings, engravings, decorations are being added to some to make them collectibles, highly prized pieces.

Are you one weapon being restored and repaired in this season? Or are you the gunsmith who is doing the work?

After I received this word from the Lord, I did some research. I had grown up around guns, gone hunting as a teenager, and knew how to shoot a gun. With refiring, refinishing, replacing stocks, barrels and so on, I was out of my league. There was a gunsmith at my childhood church who makes muskets to this day, but he wasn't accessible to quiz on these things.

Here's what I discovered: First, you disassemble the gun. (Feeling like you've been taken apart?) Then you clean it as you inspect it, and lubricate it while removing rust or corrosion. (He washes us and then anoints us with oil.) The wood stock finish is touched up if necessary and all mechanisms and the barrel are oiled. (Yeah, we all need a little spit polish now and then.) You repair the burnt or damaged parts. Factory-made pieces replace defective parts. (Deep healing happens to our heart and soul as we linger in His fire. Sometimes He removes the hardened heart and replaces it with a new one full of His love.)

Then we expand into aftermarket custom work. For gearheads, firearms aficionados and the like, this is where the chrome and craziness begin. Sling swivels, recoil pads, iron sights, scopes, these bits are all part of this custom work. Each of us is different and our process, our wilderness journey looks different from somebody else's. Some of us receive long-range scopes for sniper work and are duty weapons for law enforcement officers or the military. In the meantime, the smith can re-crown damaged muzzles on lathe, or ensure feeding bullets, ejecting and firing is fully functional. (Our ability to execute His commands will be tested.) The firearm is then test fired.

Additional points of gun fun include swapping barrels to change caliber. (When God has you pivot in your assignment, a total gear shift.) There are levels of finishing to a gun, browning, bluing and adding corrosion resistant surface layers. (This is when we develop alligator skin so the words and actions of others don't affect us; we no longer get offended or triggered so easily.) The stock maker carves the gun stocks from wood and then fits the stock to the metal. (He adds mantles, gifts, assignments to us when He deems we're ready.)

Where are the gunsmiths, the finishers, stock makers, machinists, pistol-smiths, gun engravers, custom builders/designers? Ones who build to spec from raw materials. You are needed to recondition the Body for the work ahead!

Chapter Nine

Manufacturers, Not Consumers

The Lord wants to raise up manufacturers, not consumers! He wants people who ask, "What can I give to God and others?" instead of "What can I get out of God or others?" We are to be creating, like our Father. We are to be designing, innovating, manufacturing new things to advance His kingdom on earth. Not sitting back as spectators and watching the world go to hell in a handbasket.

If you have studied the Greek words for love, you've learned about the four types: agape, eros, philo, and storge. Eros is the love of romance novels and movies, the erotic, passionate love. Philo is the love of friends and brothers. Philadelphia is known as the City of Brotherly Love for this reason. Storge is familial love, an empathetic love. And agape love is unconditional, it's God's love for mankind.

His love is more powerful than the wind, the mightiest gale, the strongest wave, the sharpest undertow current. It is tangible and brings healing.

Agape love is other-centeredness. Our lives are to be riverbeds, spilling over with love into others' lives. Enjoy the Father's love as deeply as possible, then distribute potently and widely. We are distributors of love, not manufacturers. We have a primary commodity to distribute among men, one they've never seen in the unsaved world.

We need to be filled to overflowing. You cannot give what you don't have. How do you get filled with love, with the joy of the Lord, with the peace that passes all understanding? Have you ever really thought about it?

It's not a one size fits all solution. How did He design you? What talents and gifts do you have? What is your essence? The answers to those questions will also tell you how you prefer to spend time with the Lord, how you worship.

Arthur Burk teaches about the gift of motion, explaining how some of us are designed to move. We create, innovate, inspire when we move. If you knew me growing up, you would say I definitely have this gift. When I am on the phone, I pace. I have great conversations with the Lord or friends on various video apps when walking the dog. I get ideas when I am driving. Motion is my thing.

For my readers who are the soakers, the ones who identify with Mary of Bethany, wanting to just sit at Jesus' feet and soak in His Presence. To bask in His glory. Yes, I know the Word says, "Be still and know I am God. I will be exalted among the nations." I've been learning to walk in that verse as well. There are times to just abide in Him and look upon His face. There are also times to run, to move, to dance, to jump.

The Holy Spirit just reminded me of a recent encounter during a worship service. I went to a friend for an impartation at the end of the gathering. The best way to summarize what my "word of encouragement" that morning was: a swift kick by the Audacious One to my hindparts. "Grab what's before you and go!!!" Apparently, I stalled out and started collecting dust lately. (I can hear several family members and friends shouting, "AMEN!")

Moving right along, years ago I read a book on the different styles of worship and how we were each modeled a certain way; therefore, we preferred a certain style of worship. Some felt solidarity and holiness in the liturgical style services. The rituals provided a structure that comforted them in ways others cannot comprehend. Others blossomed in a contemporary setting with upbeat music and free-flowing ways. Then you had everything in between.

Find what suits your spirit, your soul. Where do you feel connected, accepted, and part of the community? Where does your puzzle piece fit? Ask the Lord to direct your steps and to shine His light on what wounds you need to deal with in order to unify with others. Other church members have hurt many of us. We've been bitten by the sheep, kicked by the rams and ewes. And we haven't gotten over the trauma yet, which means we don't want to engage and take part in anything looking like church.

Yet, our Spirit-drenched oneness is the most important way His spectacularness is displayed in the earth. Our walking in unity and in one accord (no, not the Honda sedan) will change the world. A unified Body is a force to be reckoned with. Why do you think the enemy focuses so much on division and strife within the Body? He knows how powerful, how he'd get his own butt kicked, if we quit fighting each other and started to fight him instead.

Isn't it time to wake up to the schemes of the enemy and start fighting fire with fire?

Chapter Ten

Is There Not a Cause?

It is time to wake up to who you are, to the authority you've been given. We must go from a Kingdom of Self to Kingdom of Heaven. To eradicate separation, isolation, rejection from our hearts and minds and choose intimacy, community instead. Stop letting your current circumstance overpower the promise He gave you. Use that promise to wage war against the enemy. Step into whatever you decree. Just because you decree a thing doesn't mean you won't face opposition. We need to run into battle, to the scene because we know we hold the victory because we are seated in High Places with Jesus.

Is there not a cause? I Samuel 17:29b NKJV.

David, the shepherd boy, issued this battle cry when his eldest brother (remember David was the baby of eight boys) angrily accused him of being proud and insolent in wanting to kill Goliath. David knew his Lord God was worthy of praise and adoration. He was appalled and aggravated at this heathen's audacity to curse Yahweh. David knew God would deliver this giant into his hands.

Isn't it time we got some Holy Ghost unction beneath us to cry out in battle like David did?

We need to expect the Lord to save us, not the government or our local church or family, but God. The battle belongs to the Lord.

We should be first responders in the spirit realm. Ready to conduct spiritual first-aid to those in need. To take down the bad guy so those held captive can be liberated. We need to do like David did as a young man, to *run* into battle with Goliath. To resist the enemy and dispossess him from the land.

Stop letting your condition change your position. Shut the door to trauma and kick fear out of your mind. Fear is contagious; therefore, we need to avoid it like the plague.

Choose to work through the pain and trauma you've experienced in life and walk into freedom. Stop allowing it to dictate who you are and how you are.

Don't you realize those things happened because it was the enemy's attempt to thwart your destiny, to keep you from your calling? The perfect way to get revenge for everything you've endured is to let the Lord wash you clean of all filth and muck. To cleanse you in His blood and dip you in the Living Water. Renewed, redeemed, and revived for service in His army.

Think about it. At times, you get discouraged, Did you realize the literal meaning of that word is you have lost your courage? Where did it go? Who stole it? How do you get it back? You chase him down and accost the thief to steal it back. It is rightfully yours to begin with.

Realize, beloved, what you've been through is also about the Lord killing off your flesh so He can live in you and through you. Bill Hamon once said to welcome trials and tests as they come as if they were friends, because you know He is trying to kill your flesh so He can live in you. He wants you to be fruitful and to multiply. Bill said to employ light afflictions as workers and make them work for us. We are being transformed into His likeness, refined to reflect Him.

Listen to the testimony of others. Realize, if they can go through that, you can get through whatever you're going through.

Here are some general prophetic declarations for you to utilize. Please adapt and adjust to your own prophecies, promises, and situations.

1. I agree this new season is the next level up.
2. I agree this is an unprecedented opportunity and every step here is a victory.
3. Warring angels are with me and ready to battle with me and on my behalf.
4. I invite the seven spirits of God; the Spirit of the Lord, the Spirit of Wisdom and Understanding, the Spirit of Counsel and Might, the Spirit of Knowledge, and the Fear of the Lord to abide with me in this season of battle, at this level of intensity.
5. I choose today to step into the place my Heavenly Father has set aside for me.
6. I occupy my place on the battlefield because I have determined I want this fight.
7. I know I have been prepared and made ready for this fight.
8. The joy of the Lord is my strength. I will defend it and protect it from thievery.
9. My Lord and Savior is Jesus, Lord of Hosts, who goes with me.
10. I accept the available upgrade and accompanying acceleration.
11. I am hungry for this win.
12. I will contend to keep the ground I win.

Chapter Eleven

Unique Pieces of the Puzzle

Which puzzle piece are you?

As I mentioned earlier, each of us has unique talents, abilities, designs, and skills. We develop those abilities, gifts, and talents more fully by putting them into practice. It does no good sitting on the shelf collecting dust. Or sitting on the bench, not playing the game.

Too many believers are undercover in their church, in their workplace, and in their families. They believe in Jesus as Lord and Savior and have asked Him to redeem and renew them, but it stopped there. They are victims of arrested development. They have not allowed Jesus to come have His way inside their minds and hearts, their souls. They haven't brought him into their daily lives, asking, "What do you want to do, Lord? How can I bring you glory today?"

Most of all, they're benchwarmers.

Hold up. Wait a minute, they're not even on the bench of the ball team; they're in the stadium seats, just watching the game, berating the pitcher, yelling at the second baseman, who missed that fly ball, wondering why no one is manning third base and there's nobody in the outfield. They growl at the coach at his inability to round up a full team and play a winning game, not realizing they are the ones who should be in the field, with their hats and gloves, covering the bases and fielding the balls.

This is what 80 percent of the church is doing right now. Where did the 80 percent come from? How did I come up with that exact percentage? It's the old 80/20 rule. 20 percent of the people do 80 percent of the work. 80 percent of your revenues come from 20 percent of your customers. So forth and so on. Yes, it's a generalization, but might I challenge you to walk into church this week and determine on your own if the numbers play out there? Look at any group (online or in-person) you are involved in. It is more than likely the same way.

OK, back to the 80 percent.

So, the Lord has these folks who have God-given abilities, talents, gifts not being cultivated, sharpened or even used. That 80 percent has been given an assortment of the following gifts, but they haven't been told they have these gifts. They haven't discovered them. OR they know but they haven't learned how to use them, develop them, apply them in various situations.

The gifts are:

- Word of Knowledge
- Word of Wisdom
- Gift of Prophecy
- Gift of Faith
- Gifts of Healing
- The Working of Miracles
- Discerning of Spirit
- Different Kinds of Tongues

- Interpretation of Tongues

Let's start with the revelatory gifts: prophecy, wisdom and knowledge. I don't know if I've ever seen a time in my life when we are in more desperate need of wisdom and prophetic knowledge. Personal prophecy is to encourage, to exhort, to edify. Yes, sometimes that includes correction and discipline, but that's a whole different chapter. No bunny trails allowed. My heart aches at the number of times I have talked to fellow believers, noticing the anxiety, the depression, the fear and timidity upon them, over them. And how long they've endured this way of life.

Tell me please, how many verses exist in the Bible about fear. Not sure? Let me save you the effort of looking it up. 365 times. Seems blatantly obvious to me, Papa is giving us a verse on fear for every single day of the year.

Tell me please, what is the root of depression, anxiety and timidity? From where do they originate?

Yahweh told Joshua to be bold and courageous. Do you really think His charge to us in the Last Days is any different? I mean, really!? It is time we picked up our swords of the spirit and started kicking some hindparts of fear, anxiety, and timidity. Get your boots on. (I don't care if they're hiking boots, cowboy boots or muck boots. Just put them on your feet. Maybe muck boots would be the best, so they're easy to clean.) Got them on? Let's get to kicking.

Now then, do you not see a need for 100 percent of the Body of Christ to be exercising their revelatory gifts? To encourage, edify and exhort one another. To be in communion with the Holy Spirit, *listening*, and sharing His words with each other. What if you started edifying those in your own household, your church, your workplace, your town? What if you were a walking, living, breathing encourager, like Barnabas in the Book of Acts? What if your words of affirmation and support were the boost someone needed to move out of despair, step up out of the pity pit, launch into the goodness of God?

Many of us inside the church are discouraged, downtrodden, and desperate. What if the way to combat discouragement and hopelessness is by sharing our joys and concerns with each other? What if I stopped focusing on my own problems, issues and ailments for just a minute, and noticed you? Noticing you, I asked the Lord what He wanted me to do at the moment. I asked for the wisdom and revelation *He* wanted to share with you right then, right there. What if I stopped navel-gazing long enough to truly look at you and see you, see the burdens you are carrying and the fear in your eyes, the shame that's weighing down your shoulders, the anxiety written across your face? Then, in that moment, I listened to the Holy Spirit and shared a nugget of goodness with you that specifically addressed you in your circumstance. You would feel seen, heard, and loved. Isn't that what we all want and need today?

Years ago, I was walking through the Valley of the Shadow of Death; I was in the pit along with Joseph. Now I realize the cloud of oppression was hovering over me; it was an intense time of trials and tests. At one point of this season, I heard the audible voice of the enemy say, "Why are you crying out to Jesus? He doesn't love you anyway." As a child who grew up knowing and loving the Lord, this concept was foreign to me and rocked me to my core. I fell to the floor and wept.

Within minutes, my phone rang, and a friend called to set my mind right, without knowing what was going on. Afterward, the Lord gently whispered, "Why would you even believe that worm? You *know* better."

Around this time, I was talking to a spiritual father, who told me, "What you're going through isn't about you. It's about being able to help others once you get through it."

The light bulb switched on and I came back to life. "Oh, hold on now. I need to get the victory here so I can help others walk out their own victories. This ain't about me. It's about me being equipped and trained so I can empower and encourage others."

That simple word of wisdom totally shifted my battle. The Holy Spirit knew what I needed to hear and when. How much longer would I have been stuck under that cloud of oppression if he hadn't given a small word of wisdom in the moment? It's definitely something to think about, and a good enough reason for you to step out and say what the Holy Spirit is prompting you to say, any time and any place.

Moving on, the gifts of power, faith, healing and miracle working are among this group. My grandmother walked in amazing faith and inspired me to do the same. I am so grateful for her legacy of faith. But first, let me tattle on my husband to give you a simple example of the gift of faith in action.

Several years ago, we were having lunch together during a workday at my favorite Mediterranean restaurant in Hagerstown, Maryland. As we cleaned off our table and walked out, I greeted a friend of mine who was dining with two other women. I could tell Rob had heard a word from the Lord for the youngest at the table and gently nudged him to share. He had been having an intense moment of fellowship with the Holy Spirit about whether he was to talk to the girl. I did not know what he had heard, but knew she needed to hear it. (After being married for twenty-plus years, you learn to recognize when the Holy Spirit is talking to your spouse, when He's telling him to do or say something and there's some kickback happening. You recognize the twitch, the look in the eye, the grimace, the non-verbals!)

Rob stopped and quietly said, "I don't know what's going on, but I do know that God has it, and it will all work out. Just trust Him." Or something along those lines.

She started crying, and my friend looked at us. "That is so on point. You have no idea."

Just a simple sentence to encourage her. No need to go deeper or more detailed. Just a bit of sunshine on a cloudy day. He took the time to share his faith with her, just when hers needed a boost.

Now let's talk about what happens to you when you release a prophetic word. Aside from being a conduit of His glory and grace, there comes a feeling of completion, an increase of faith, an affirmation of a fulfilled prophecy cannot be explained. To speak out what we sense within our spirits, to call it forth, to foretell of the future and then see it take place.

Onto one of my favorites, the gift of healing. I mean, Joan Hunter is the one who ordained me; I get it honestly from one of my spiritual mothers.

I just love to pray for people and see God show up. There's just something about praying with someone to see their breakthrough manifest, and it happens. I have seen blind eyes open, the mute speak, the lame walk. I have seen shoulder bursitis healed instantly; granted, they first relinquished burdens they carried that weren't theirs, THEN the healing came. I have seen faces light up when depression and anxiety were broken off.

The working of miracles is a gift I believe of which the Body of Christ has barely seen the tip of the iceberg. I feel we are entering a season where the redeemed of the Lord will walk in supernatural signs and wonders the world has yet to even see. Jesus said we would do greater things than He did. We have *NOT* been walking in that yet.

One fun miracle story I have is about water and a book. If you know me personally, I know you're not surprised a book is in this story. A business client of mine had given me his book on Disney Leadership called *Creating Magic*. I had it, a bottle of water, and some papers in my tote bag one morning as I walked into my office. I sat my bag on an office chair and then went over to my desk and got to work.

After a few hours, I got thirsty and went to the bag to extract my water bottle. Evidently, I had taken a sip during my commute to work and failed to shut the lid. The bottle had tipped over inside the bag and there were several inches of water in the bag's bottom. I immediately cringed, realizing the book would be water damaged and I'd have to buy a replacement book for my friend. I grabbed the book and pulled it out of the bag to examine the damage.

IT WAS BONE DRY.

I flipped it all around, but there was no evidence it had been immersed in water at all.

I showed it to my assistant and told her what had happened. She laughed and remarked, "It *is* called *Creating Magic.*"

I told her God was showing off.

It is time to walk on water, to see ax heads float, to multiply loaves and fishes.

Then we have the Gifts of Inspiration: prophecy, diverse tongues and interpretation of tongues. Religious people have widely debated these gifts, falsely used and mistreated them. It is time for them to be redeemed, cleansed, and exercised in honorable fashion. Part of prophecy is dream interpretation. The spirit realm is speaking to us all the time in our dreams. It is one language of God. It's time we learned to speak it and discern what He is saying to us.

Not all dreams come from the Lord, some are from the enemy and others are from our soulish desires. As we reflect on the dreams, the Lord can speak to us. Journaling our dreams and asking Him for interpretation shows Him we value His way of speaking and want to hear Him. Streams Ministries is a great resource for learning about how to interpret your dreams. John Thomas recently released a new book, *Dream Elements: An Alternative Dream Dictionary*, with QR codes hidden in it, which link to videos explaining that element in greater detail. What a fascinating idea!

We make prophecy way more complicated than it must be. I once was in a prophetic activation at a conference, paired with a stranger. All I heard was the name Deborah. I told her the name and said, "That's all I heard, all I have to give." She started crying and said it was a confirmation of what God had been saying to her for months. He was calling her to be like Deborah, the judge. She had questioned Him whether she was really hearing from Him, or it was all made up. I didn't need to know anything else or say anything else. One name was enough for her in that season, that moment. She didn't need me to say anything else.

Speaking in tongues and interpreting tongues are two gifts where we need to walk in holiness and righteousness. And then let the Holy Spirit flow. Stop getting all religious about the gift. Instead, seek the Lord and talk to Him about it.

When you are baptized in the Holy Spirit, you receive a prayer language. If you're stubborn and a bit controlling, like I was, it might take a few weeks or even years for this to happen. You might even find yourself coming to after a moment of glory on the floor during a worship service, stuttering, and stumbling in a new language.

As you pray in tongues, you edify yourself (1 Corinthians 14:4), your spirit is encouraged. You allow the Holy Spirit to pour into you and out of you. The Spirit can say what He wants in the moment. You may speak in a heavenly language or an earthly language someone else may understand.

The enemy doesn't like when you pray in tongues and will fight hard against you doing so because he knows its impact. Recognize it is a gift and ask the Father for it and then use it regularly. Think of it like a muscle; don't let it atrophy from lack of use.

Jesus said, "And these signs will accompany those who believe: In my name they will drive out demons; they will speak in new tongues" (Mark 16:17).

In a group setting, one who prays in another tongue can be understood by someone else in the room. It is for the edification and faith building of others. Just as that day in Acts, when the people in the street heard the disciples speaking in their home languages, yet the disciples did not know that language in the natural realm.

Paul said in 1 Cor. 14:5, I would like every one of you to speak in tongues. When we speak in tongues, we speak to God, not man (1 Corinthians 14:2). We praise Him. We declare His wonders and majesty (Acts 2:11). We do not know what we ought to pray for, but the Spirit himself intercedes for us with groans that words cannot express ...because the Spirit intercedes for the saints in accordance with God's will (Romans 8:26-27). I don't know about you, but I have times when I just don't even know how to speak, what to say. I can't put anything into words. (I know, I know. That is hard for some of you to fathom: me not having the words to say, but it happens.) It is so good to know, in those moments, I can hit my knees and just pray in the Spirit, knowing He hears me and holds me close.

Chapter Twelve

Got Bait?

We are all one-of-a-kind masterpieces, not created by accident, endowed with the favor of God. It's not meant to be kept inside of us. Remember Romans 11:29: the gifts and callings of God are irrevocable. These gifts are given to equip and empower others. We are talented, skilled, and designed with a purpose.

That purpose is not sitting still in the back of the church, or on the sofa watching the preacher man on TV. I don't care if your hands are in the air and you're shouting amen every Sunday.

It is time to get off your rump and make something thump. The time for sitting back and watching has ended. There is an ongoing battle for our attention, the affections of our heart. We need to engage fully and fight back. It's time to storm the gates of hell with water pistols.

Our goal, our aim, is to move consistently in harmony with each other and Jesus. We need to realize it is not about us, our talents, our experiences, our expertise, our knowledge or abilities. Instead, it is all about Jesus, His glory, the mysteries of God being revealed, His love, His Kingdom coming on earth, His Presence being seen and felt across the globe.

As John Bevere teaches, the bait of satan is offense. We have been taking on offenses, wounds, and burdens for far too long, generations even. It's time to walk in grace and mercy, to love another, letting our skin thicken, so little foxes don't steal the grapes off the vines anymore. Could we grow up and grow past this getting offended at being looked at crosswise? I mean seriously.

We've become offended by our brother, against our neighbor, our spouse, our parents, anyone and everyone. We cannot feel peace; we cannot be overcome with joy because we're too offended.

How do you know if you have swallowed the bait? I'm glad you asked. If you're carrying bitterness, resentment, grudges, offense, you've taken the bait of Satan. Literally power bait. I used to use powerbait when trout fishing in Pennsylvania with my father. There were multiple colors, all fluorescent in shade, neon green, chartreuse, pink, orange in these cool little jars.

You, beloved, have eaten the bait; hook, line and sinker. Now bitterness, the roots of pain, trauma, the experiences you've been through, are coursing through your veins. Wounds haven't healed because you're still resentful and harboring grudges. This means you still expect the same reaction, treatment again and again. You have a bitter root expectation. Often this can manifest in your body as arthritis, lower back pain, endometriosis, cardiac issues, cancer and more. (I suggest checking out Henry Wright's book *A More Excellent Way* and Joan Hunter's *Healing the Whole Man Handbook* for more research-backed information on the spiritual impact on our natural bodies.)

You might resent your abuser, the one who mistreated you, physically assaulted you, even raped you. Which is totally understandable. Maybe you resent all men, pastors, women, supervisors, authority figures, male relatives, friends, and so on because someone in their field, their gender, their profession, betrayed you, hurt you, abused you. You don't connect well with others. You are not truly intimate with anyone, even God, because of the walls of self-protection you've erected around your heart. There is no communion with anyone because of the bitterness, the resentment you're holding onto. Someone has stolen your joy; smothered your dreams to death.

You inwardly shout, "What about me? This happened to me. Why should I let it go? Why should I trust again? Why? Can you tell me it won't happen again? Man's already proven they can't be trusted...."

I know the moves. I know the battle stance we take against our own brothers and sisters. We think the walls in our hearts and souls protect us. I know because I've walked this walk myself.

Let me just tell you, self-preservation, self-protection is a prison, a dungeon holding you captive. And you don't even know it yet. The walls you've erected out of the hurt, the damage that was done, are now keeping out the One who loves you more than you'll ever know. The walls prevent your Redeemer from coming close, from touching the very points where you hurt the most and being able to heal them, restoring you to wholeness.

The walls are the sides of your prison cell. You've built your own cell with the bricks of doubt, fear of man, fear of failure, fear of lack, fear of success, fear of not being perfect, not being good enough. Bricks of distrust, resentment, hatred, doubt, discord are all laid together to construct your prison. Self-hatred, self-loathing, self-rejection, self-sabotage make up the masonry glue holding them together. This turtle-like shell you've covered your heart with doesn't protect you from hurt, from heartache, from trauma. It only holds the past inside. All the trauma, pain, disasters you've already survived are being kept inside, stored inside your heart, because you won't let anyone else in for fear you'll hurt more.

Beloved, your joy is your strength. The dark one has stolen yours. The Risen Savior comes now, riding on the clouds. His eyes are piercing with Glory Fire. His Living Water fracks through the shell you've kept yourself in, thinking it protected you. The water flows through the cracks, shattering it to pieces.

Love breaks in.

Glory ignites an all-consuming fire deep inside of you, burning anything off not of Him.

Beloved child, it's time to realize you were made for so much more. You were born to connect, to create, to commune with Him and others. You were designed to be full of joy, peace and love. It's time to let go of the world's ways, grudges, judgments, criticisms, expectations and let Jesus and His angels in. Allow them to come and have their way in you.

It's time to tear down the walls. Let *LOVE* in. It's time to allow Jesus to be your protector, knowing He has given His angels charge over you.

Finding where you fit in, your tribe requires connection. It takes *you* getting involved, engaging, participating,taking a seat at the table. You have to do something. Change your standard operating procedure of shutting everyone out. Shift from the gear of rejection to the gear of love and acceptance. The first thing you have to do is look in the mirror and see who you see. Accept that person as is and love yourself.

Stop allowing guilt and shame to rule your life. Either Jesus' death on that Cross was enough to redeem you or it was a complete waste.

You are redeemed and forgiven, given new robes of righteousness to wear. Break out of your shell and you'll see breakthroughs occur in your life.

The manifestation of breakthroughs actually starts with forgiveness. Forgiveness disentangles you from the offender's trauma and torment. Forgiveness is not letting the abuser, the tormentor, the sinner get away with his crime, her sin. By forgiving them, you are not saying it's okay that it happened. You don't condone the behavior, the actions. You release them to Jesus so you can realize the truth of the scripture: He forgives us as we forgive others. Forgiveness means you give the Holy Spirit permission to come into your heart, your mind, your soul and bring healing to the wounds caused by the pain and trauma of what happened. It means you're willing to let go of the right to be angry and choose to embrace the right to be free instead.

See the prayers for forgiving others and self in the **Appendix** for guidelines on how to walk this out.

Beloved, deal with your own issues, your own triggers, your own stuff. When something gets in your crawl, gets under your skin, stop. Do not engage. Do not scream, yell and shout. Do not growl, grumble and mumble. Shut your mouth. Take a deep breath. Now, with your lips buttoned like a good kid, look to your Heavenly Father and ask, "Papa, what is it about this situation, this person, this moment that is agitating me like a good washing machine? Why am I so freaked out over this? Why?" Be still. *Listen.* See what He has to say.

Beloved, as we experience inner healing, as we allow Jesus to dig deep, uproot those weeds that have been growing in our soul gardens for decades, maybe even generations, and allow Him to shake the earth from those roots, tossing them into the fire, we get to experience more freedom. The more we surrender, the more we open up, asking for Him to shine His light on whatever He wants for as long as He wants, the more we find ourselves walking in greater freedom. Yet we are the ones who have to make the choice. We have to say we are sick and tired of being sick and tired. We realize the Rolling Stones nailed it with their "I can't get no satisfaction" song when we think about trying to do life in the flesh, on our own, in our own strength.

Do you know your identity, your giftings, your talents? Have you accepted them, accepted yourself just as God made you? Isn't it time you did? Beloved, do you realize, when you know who you are, God shows up even grander? You are a missionary, a minister. You walk into dark places daily. Schools, offices, stores. There are people who don't know Jesus. The culture where you work, live, and play is not Kingdom culture. You are an ambassador of heaven sent to your work site, to your school, your family. It's time to live like one.

He will put you in places that place a healthy demand on what's inside of you. He wants to draw it out of you. The Godhead did not design you to be self-sufficient. Others rely on you, and you rely on others to complete the puzzle of life. It is time to unlock the potential of God's nature inside of you. You are a resource for others. He gives to you so you can plant the seed and see it grow, develop into a source of provision, a continuous stream for you and others. Nations will come to you to get what they need. The roots go deep, so the tree grows tall and strong. It becomes a legacy.

We are to be the most empowered, ingenuous, resourced people on the earth. It is time to stop being ashamed of the gospel. We should be change agents for the Lord, leaders of the shift happening globally.

Chapter Thirteen

Unity

There will be unity among My children, My believers outside the church first. In the workplace, in groups, in non-church ministries, in running groups, business centers, schools and other non-religious settings. My believers will come together wherever they are and align into My army, to unite as one. Like magnets, they are being pulled supernaturally to each other, fitting together like a puzzle. I have a grand plan and a design in mind as I fit the pieces together. Gifts, styles, abilities have been assessed and now are being combined into teams, into groups who glorify Me in their actions.

The enemy has focused on spreading division, strife, chaos and confusion inside the Body for centuries. My people have been clueless to the tactics and antics of the enemy long enough. They have allowed the seeds of confusion and division to grow in their soil, rather than uprooting them at first sight. You must realize walking with a critical heart, a judging stance, a cynical mindset is being orphan-spirited and not in alignment with Me.

Jumping on trains of thought that berate, belittle and criticize others takes you away from My Presence. Choose to focus on what is good, holy, pure and righteous instead.

There is power, wonder-working power when you align with others. Other religions grasp this concept easily and exercise it regularly. They fast together, chant together, worship together, knowing their power and influence increases as they come together in agreement.

Yet My own Church has failed to grasp this basic concept. My Son said, where two or three are gathered, there He is in their midst. That He is exalted among their praises. Breakthrough happens when YOU come into agreement with My Will and each other. When you align with My plumb-line and walk in My ways, you will see an acceleration take place.

Learn to recognize the tactics of the enemy and rebuke him immediately. Choose unity and alignment. Watch how I move on your behalf.

SET ASIDES

This is My remnant, pure ones, the sanctified. Those who always stood out from the crowd, who never quite fit in, have been set aside for My purpose in this season.

Let me explain what set asides are. You may have heard prophetic words about people being set aside for a future purpose. You may have been told that is specifically you. Did you know there is a procurement program in the US government called set asides? This program ensures small businesses get a portion of the work.

The federal government prefers to contract with small businesses whenever possible. Contracting officials can use set-aside and sole-source contracts to help their agencies meet their small business contracting goals. If there is a small business who can provide the product or service at a fair and reasonable price, the contract can be solely sourced to that company, instead of being put out for competitive bid. This allows small businesses to compete with larger corporations that typically get all of the work.

Categories include: women-owned small business, small disadvantaged business and 8a, historically underutilized business zones, service-disabled veteran owned small business.

Each department has a portion of contracting business with a set-aside designation for small businesses. They are held accountable each year to reach their goals. This way the major large company contractors do not monopolize all the government work. I used to have a job where I would host workshops for small businesses to connect with federal and state procurement officers to discover opportunities for their businesses.[1]

Just as the US government designates portions of its work and funding for a specially designated group of businesses, the Lord has set aside treasures, glory, awards, favors, recognition, revelation, answers for His children in this season. There are hidden treasures in these moments for you to discover. You are chosen, set aside for His purposes. Therefore, He has set aside blessing and honor for you as you fulfill the purpose for which He created you. As you walk out your destiny, you discover Him and He brings goodness and mercy into your life.

Comparison

Comparison will distract you from the *best* God has for you. You have a unique fingerprint, a calling that doesn't look like anyone else's calling. Your destiny is specific to you. Your talents, your abilities, your experiences, your DNA combine to make you into the person God wants you to be so you can advance His Kingdom on earth in your special way.

Your life is your own. It will not resemble or mimic another person's life.

1. "Set-aside procurement.: SBA. October 21, 2022. https://www.sba.gov/partners/contracting-officials/small-business-procurement/set-aside-procurement.

Learn to celebrate with others. Learn to get excited about what God is doing in them and through them. Stop saying, "What about me?" You are in a different stage of life, a different season, and a process. Your process may not look like your friend's. It should not.

Your identity, your value are found in Jesus alone. Choose to celebrate the joys and successes of others. Accept that your value and identity are not in WHAT you do, but WHO you are in Him.

As you step into what He has prepared for you, your calling, your assignment, know your support system, your tribe, your mentors have your back. You take the lead and know they are following you into the future. They will endorse you, support you, and push you. Mentors specifically push you where you resist going.

Feeling like you're not ready to go? Wondering if you can step out? Beloved, it's time to tell the enemy he can't treat you like that anymore. Tell the cloud of oppression over you to *move.*

There are people whose blessings, whose healing and deliverance are locked up in your calling, your authority. You are the carrier of others' deliverance, their promises fulfilled, their victories. You stepping out in faith is actually the key to someone else getting free.

As a Body, we've been in survival mode for far too long. Think about it. Systems shut down when the focus is on survival. If a woman is anorexic, her menstrual cycle stops because she isn't taking in enough calories to survive. She loses certain body functions due to streamlining in order to stay alive. The Body of Christ has been fighting ground warfare for so long, not consuming enough of the Bread of Life, we have shut down functions in order to just stay alive.

It is time to stop just surviving and start thriving in this life. To walk from victory, not to it. To see the Body of Christ in good health and abundance, not sick, disabled, and debilitated.

In order to thrive, we need to breathe. We need to breathe in the Ruach breath of life.

Chapter Fourteen

Breath of Life

The Lord has given us His breath. He wants us to breathe life into our situations. Into the valley of dry bones in our lives. We shouldn't be waiting on Him to do it. He created the universe with His words, with His exhale. What are we speaking forth, creating with our own words? Let there be ____. His breath in us means we can decree a thing into existence. We should use His Word as our asthma inhaler. We breathe in the Word of God daily to cleanse our bodies, minds and souls.

Want someone to change? Speak forth the change. Call what isn't as though it is. Speak it into existence. Call them into their destiny. Now, don't get twisted in this. I'm not talking about controlling and witchcraft. We are not to do that. I'm talking about speaking blessing and life over yourself, your family, your coworkers.

I see the puppy-dog head cock of misunderstanding on your face. Allow me to give an example. "I decree shalom over my family. Over my husband's mind, his heart, his soul, I decree Shalom. I speak peace over this house. Nothing missing. Nothing lacking. Nothing broken. I thank You, Lord, that You are a good Father and You give excellent gifts. I thank You that my husband is a good provider, a kindhearted and gentle warrior of Yours. I thank You that he is blessed going out and coming in. I thank You that You determine every one of our days. We can sow seeds of Kingdom change and goodness through divine appointments. I thank You for connections and provision coming from Your hills. I thank You for good health and cancel every attack of witchcraft or curse coming against my family right now in Jesus' name. You are holy and worthy of all praise. In Jesus' name, Amen."

Too many of us have been praying witchcraft prayers, not realizing what we were doing. We prayed for the person to change, to cut his hair, to take the job you prefer, to do what *you* want her to do. We did not respect their free will, their boundaries. This is witchcraft and not godly praying. It is time for the Body of Christ to stop doing that. We need to seek the Godhead and ask what His will is. Then we pray into that, not our own will. Which college does He want your child to attend, not necessarily your alma mater? Which job is the right one?

Now is the time to walk in righteousness, to choose rightly, even in our prayers. His Word says the righteous flourish like a palm tree. Category 1 hurricanes do not uproot them. You know, the lowest level of a hurricane, barely even categorized as a hurricane, with winds under 95 mph. They hold fast with deep roots, bending and swaying with the wind.

We focus on our situation, our circumstances. Amid an intense season, a painful moment, a fiery trial, if we lack maturity in Christ, our go-to move, our default stance is one where we are focused on the problem, on what's wrong, according to our perspective. We yell at God, argue with Him, ignore Him, run to every person we know to discuss the matter except the One who could really help.

We need to look to the One who created us, destined us for greatness, who allowed this moment, this test in our life to mold us, to break us, to prune us, to polish us. To step out of the chaos, confusion and drama for a minute and step into our high place where we are seated with Jesus. We are to seek His Face and ask what He is doing in the moment. What does He want us to learn amid this? Who is Yahweh for us right now? Provider? Healer? Protector? Lord of Hosts? Each trial, each test provides an opportunity to learn a new facet of the Lord, discover additional aspects and features of Him.

Life is about process. We focus on our destination, where we want to go, the place, the position where we think life will be just dandy. And we ignore, we neglect the process, the journey we take to get there. Yet that's the joy of life, that's where treasures from heaven are hidden, waiting for you to discover them.

Maturity means we look to Heaven during chaos, turmoil and drama. "What are You doing? Who are You for me in this moment? How can I join You in Your work here? What do You want me to do right here, right now? How do I change my perspective, obtain a new lens to view things?"

And then silently wait for Him to answer.

That's one key to abundant Life in Christ.

Chapter Fifteen

Real Talk from the Battlefront

(Brace yourself. Your Drill Sergeant from Army Basic Training or Navy Boot Camp has just taken the microphone.)

Buck up, buttercup. No one ever promised you a rose garden. Life ain't all peaches and cream. Some people are harsh, mean, and angry. They are not looking out for you. They mean to harm you or at least win at your expense. They don't care if you succeed or not. They have listened to the lies of the enemy for far too many years. The bitterness and resentment have settled deeply in their souls. Selfishness, self-centeredness, even narcissism are rampant in our world today. They need to see the goodness and mercy of God. Any hope of change comes from the intervention of kindness and love.

This means you. Focus on doing what you need to do to get the job done well. Get over the tone of voice in the article, the statement, the comment. Just review it, read it and deal with it. Chew the meat and spit out the bones. Apply yourself properly. Remain in your Shalom Zone of love, joy, and peace. Know you are surrounded by glory and angels, ready to assist and protect. Don't get caught up in ground warfare. Do not succumb to the enemy's strategies to keep you from your assignment.

We all need to get over ourselves and get to advancing the Kingdom. While we're at it, we need to grow up. The Lord needs warriors who are ready for the fight, not ones who are still in the practice room, trying to figure out how to hold the sword.

Stop behaving as if you were a spiritual toddler. No more milky for you. Preachers and teachers have spoon-fed you for far too long. You expect church leadership to dissect, distill, digest the Word of God for you, and then regurgitate it for you to eat, just like baby birds in the nest.

Hey, eaglet, it's time to fly. You know those things on your sides with feathers? They're wings, designed to soar on wind currents. Let's go. It's time to get things done.

I mean it. Quit worrying about who said what and which sheep in the fold is really a wolf and focus on your own work.

Seriously.

Whining never changed the world. It is high time we stopped justifying our fears and started doing something with the gifts and talents we've been given. Stop coddling each other. We need to grab ahold of the man we're wrestling with and ask for a blessing.

Go after your God dream with everything you got, regardless of man's reaction to you.

Chapter Sixteen

Skeletal Alignment

So much of My Church today is operating on its own. They are out of alignment with the Head, Jesus Christ. A Holy Ghost chiropractic adjustment is happening across the globe as the Body of Christ is brought into alignment with Her Head. The skeletal system provides structure and protection to the rest of the body. Systems, organs, functions, all operate optimally when the bones are in alignment.

Nerves and muscles pinch, they hurt when bones don't line up. My children are aching and in pain because of the misalignment in the Church.

The structure of the Church in operation presently is not based on MY *design. It is not heaven-sent and based on the blueprints I developed several millennia ago. Man has corrupted and contaminated what I started centuries ago. Pride, greed, arrogance, control and manipulation have reigned inside the Church for far too long. They are the pillars that hold up the building. Man has taken what My Son birthed at the Cross and marred its very face. Multiple layers, reporting structures, fees to be paid ... all of that was never My intention for My ekklesia.*

My design is based on love, based on loyalty, based on honor. I want the Body to look like family, to look like an army. To resemble My Friend's, Abraham's, family when he walked the earth. He had men, women and children in his household, his tribe, who were not of his bloodline. They were people who journeyed through life as a large family. They served together, ate together, and fought together. This tribe of wanderers defeated the kings of their land, bringing honor to their lord, Abraham. Abraham had 318 trained men who chased down four *kings' armies. These men were trained by him, born in his house. Do you understand the significance of one tribe overcoming four armies at once? Think about it.*

Grab your Bible and let's dive into Genesis 14. Apparently there was an ongoing rebellion in the Valley of Siddim (full of tar pits) while Lot was living in Sodom. Four kings were fed up with being subject to Kedorlaomer, King of Elam, and his allies. The rebel forces looted Sodom and Gomorrah, stole all the food and kidnapped Lot as well as his possessions. A lone escapee reports the attack to Abram, sparking an immediate response by Abram to rally a posse to go after them. During the night, he split his men and attacked, chasing them as far as Hobah. He and his tribe recovered all the goods and brought back Lot, his possessions *and other people.*

A tribe, a community led by Yahweh's friend, Abraham, went after an allied force of multiple armies and subdued them, recovered what was lost. This wasn't a large force, a bunch of subjects, serfs, or slaves. It was a family who did life together and defended each other. A family who loved well.

The foundation of a healthy, Christ-like community is love. Jesus said in the gospels we would be known as His followers because of our love, love for others, This starts by being filled with the love of God, letting it flow into every nook and cranny of our hearts and souls. He is ready to do so.

I am filling you with 100 percent pure love. Straight from the Throne Room, pure love. Flooding every cell, every organ, every system with 100 percent pure love. It cures what ails you. It washes you, cleanses you anew. There is a waterfall of love over you. It is crashing over you, drenching you in My love. Do you hear Me, child? Completely covered, thoroughly filled with My love.

I am filling you with more of My love so you can walk in love everywhere you go. Be filled more fully with My Love so you can walk in love everywhere you go. I want you to put love before you, extend My love out in front of you as a guard, as a shield. You have a new weapon, child, a shield of love.

As you raise your shield to block incoming attacks, love blocks it all out. Nothing can penetrate My love. No attack can conquer My Love. My Love quenches every fiery dart, flaming arrows, missiles of fear, grenades of doubt, rockets of anger, bombs of hesitation — they are all vanquished with My love.

Your fallback, your go-to is now My love. When the enemy comes, My love responds like a flood. Washing away everything meant to harm you, to hurt you.

You are being recalibrated to a new frequency. You are being reset to your original design, love, joy and peace.

It is synchronization time. It is time for My ekklesia to coordinate their watches to the exact second. It is time for balance and consonance, for harmony and coherence in the Body. As they come into alignment with My plumbline and each other, acceleration will take place. They will synchronize their lives with My divine purpose in THIS hour.

When the Body of Christ walks in unity, it releases heaven to come to earth.

In My tribe, members know their identities and their assignments. They don't squander resources and they steward My gifts well. They are loyal to each other and Me. They defend their own and go on the offensive when necessary. When specific skills or talents are needed, the craftsman appears. No need for jealousy or control. Instead, they appreciate and honor each other's abilities with ease. They go where they are sent to accomplish My will, to perform My work.

Experienced ones equip and train the young ones, the new ones in how to utilize their talents and skills for My Kingdom. They are taught how to hear My voice and walk with confidence.

I am releasing angels of unity and alignment upon My Church in this season. Chaos, discord, division, offense have been allowed to run amok inside My Church long enough. I decree unity, reconciliation, redemption and alignment are coming as a tsunami wave across the globe. Watch and see what happens between My children in this season. Walls are being torn down by these angels. Dams are being released. Strongholds are coming down as these angels work among My church.

The foundation, the plumbline, and the structure of a building are all tested by stress. I am testing the very foundation of the Church to show the world who I really am. What is not of Me is being removed. To reveal Truth to the nations.

It is time to be about relationship. It's about the relationship with Papa and each other. Not functionality. You cannot take possession of what you don't believe. You need to believe what God says about you. See yourself how HE sees you. To know you have a Father and you have come home. It is time to party! It's time to live the life worth the travailing of the intercessors and warriors who went before us.

Chapter Seventeen

Becoming Who We Are

In *Revolution Within*, Dwight Edwards defines the church as: "a network of diverse individuals whose lives are so beautifully interconnected that it's nothing short of stunning. Their specialty: a relational excellence that unmistakably reflects the love within and between the Trinity."

He continues, "The world sees Christ more clearly when His love flows freely among believers." Hebrews 10:24 TPT describes this free flow of love as:

"Discover creative ways to encourage others and to motivate them toward acts of compassion, doing beautiful works as expressions of love."

According to Dwight, stir up means to incite, stimulate, create a fever. Who stirs you up? Who strengthens your hand in God as Jonathan did David? Who kindles the embers within your soul when they've all but gone out? Who incites you to walk into your destiny, to fulfill your purpose on earth?

Dwight shares how the "New Covenant arouses hope, confident expectation and blazing optimism. It seeks to arouse the godly inclination in all believers to know God more deeply, to hunger for His best, to move forward in His power to the only way of life that can genuinely satisfy their new hearts. Our lives are to have the fragrance of God all over them. View others in light of their potential, not their problems."

We are "designed to be exhibitors of the supernatural, a reflection of His craftsmanship. Helping others hear the voice of God for themselves and find their unique God-designed, God-given calling."

It is time we "release what God already has set in motion." We need to take a stance beside each other, saying, "Know I am relentlessly and unconditionally for you. I see your potential for the Kingdom of God and it excites me. I'll do all I can to help see this purpose realized. I'll do all I can to help inflame your new nature. I'll also stand against your flesh when necessary."

Keep a pulse on your peace. You're the only one fighting for it. ~Justin Carpenter

As you are walking through your day, notice what happens. What steals your joy, attacks your peace, sideswipes your patience with one action or word? Is it the grumbling by your children, the fact your spouse left his shoes by his chair instead of putting them away? Is it the driver who cut you off as you drove to work? Is it someone's comment on your social media post that just does it for you?

Assess. Ascertain what's happening. (Hold up. I just realized we needed to set the scene for where we are having this conversation right now. You're at my board table in the War Room and we're having a battle strategy session regarding your life and assignment here on earth. Yes, Jesus, Father, Holy Spirit and some of the great cloud of witnesses are here. Of course, your angels are meandering about, getting new assignments and tools for battle as we plan.) Back to reviewing your day, your week. Let's review your day and determine where the thievery is occurring.

Graham Cooke has taught for years on staying centered on peace and battling from a place of rest. I can feel the atmosphere shift just by turning on one of his prophetic soaking sessions. Graham explained years ago how we needed to be stabilized in Shalom, the peace of the Lord. When something happened to rob him of his peace, he trained himself to find his way back to it. Not simply let that circumstance, the thing to ruin his day, to throw him into a tailspin.

How many of us get caught up in the drama and take hours if not days to realize our joy is gone, our peace has left the station? As BB King used to sing, "The Thrill Is Gone," baby. How quickly do you realize it's gone? Are you so wrapped around the axle about the thing, you don't even know where you are or who are you anymore? You're fired up and breathing fire upon anyone who dares to come close. As Jesus told the Sons of Thunder, "You know not what spirit you are of."

As we transform into His likeness, we become like ducks and learn to let things just roll off our backs. Don't react. Don't engage. Just walk away. Just extend grace and mercy. Let it go and hold onto your peace, your joy instead. Then watch to see how your days change for good.

Let's talk about who you really are and maybe then you'll comprehend why letting small stuff get to you is not worth it.

Chapter Eighteen

Comparison & Identity

Identity. Mistaken identity. Stolen identity. Gender identity. There is so much discussion around identity as the world sees it daily, and yet most believers really do not know their own. They know their names, their worldly identities, but they are clueless with their Kingdom Identities. Asking the questions: Who are you? What is your identity? ends up with answers about what they do and who their family members are, not about their life purpose, their destiny on this earth.

When a much-loved child of God discovers who she is in Christ, develops his own identity statements and really *gets* who he is, how Heaven sees him, there is a shift in the atmosphere and the world takes notice.

Just stop.

Stop comparing yourself with others. Comparisons, competitions, contests are not of Me. There is no good found in them.

You were created to love Me, to serve Me, to worship Me. You were designed differently, given different talents, different gifts, different skills. The world has yet to see one just like you.

You were made to stand out, to differ from the rest. You are Mine. Rest in Me. Abide in Me. Just relax. Be still. Quit striving. Quit chasing af-

ter man's approval, man's appreciation, worldly education and acclaims. They will never teach you what you yearn to know. They will never fill the hole inside of you designed to cause you to yearn, to seek, to ask for more, to pursue, to explore, to chase after.

Realize what you yearn for, what you desire intensely is ME. All of Me, my love, My peace, My joy, My provision, My grace, goodness. I am closer than your next breath. I am deep within you. I am all you need. I will teach you. I will show you everything you need to know, everything – just rest in Me. As you abide, as you fall into Me, I reveal the mysteries of the deep. There are so many treasures I've hidden for your discovery. You simply need to seek them out, to focus on more of Me and not the world.

Fall into Me. I have so much more for you. I have your inheritance waiting for you. Come. Just come.

It is time for the sons and daughters of the King to arise and shine (Isaiah 60:1) It is time for them to walk in the fullness of who they really are, to walk into their identities.

First, let's start with Merriam Webster's definition of identity.

> The definition is a) who someone is; the name of a person b) the qualities, beliefs, etc., that make a particular person or group different. 1. A: sameness of essential or generic character in different instances. B: sameness in all that constitutes the objective reality of a thing; ONENESS. 2. A: the distinguishing character or personality of an individual: individuality. B: the relation established by psychological identification. 3. The condition of being the same with something described or asserted <establish the *identity* of stolen goods>. 4. An equation that is satisfied for all values of the symbols.

Notice these parts of the definition: the essential character, the distinguishing character of a person. What makes you, well, you. Just as your fingerprint, your DNA does not match anyone else's, your identity is your own and does not completely match anyone else. Your purpose in the Kingdom is *NOT* the same as anyone else's. So stop comparing yourself with those around you, with those you see online or on TV. Just stop it. It's pointless. Stop being distracted from your purpose, your destiny with the comparison game and focus on why you are here, what your assignment is. Enough already. We have too much work to do for such nonsense.

Let me guess what you are thinking now. "OK, fine then. I *won't* compare myself to others anymore. Happy now? But what is my assignment? What am I supposed to be doing instead? What *work* are you talking about?"

Or something along those lines. I am so glad you asked. Let's talk about that.

Discovering your identity, your life purpose, starts with focusing on *WHOSE* you are and *WHO* He is. (Right now, as I write this, Way Maker by Sinach is playing on my playlist on Amazon Music. If you haven't heard this song before, venture over to your favorite source of online music and find it. It's *that* good.) Now, where were we? Talking about who God is. His traits. His characteristics. His attributes. His names. His titles.

- El Shaddai (Lord God Almighty)
- El Elyon (The Most High God, Sovereign)
- El Roi (He sees you)
- El Kanna (Jealous God)
- Abba (My Daddy)
- Adonai (Lord, Master)
- Yahweh (Lord, Jehovah)
- Jehovah Nissi (The Lord My Banner)

- Jehovah Raah (The Lord My Shepherd)
- Jehovah Rapha (The Lord That Heals)
- Jehovah Shammah (The Lord Is There)
- Jehovah Jireh (The Lord My Provider)
- Jehovah Shalom (The Lord of Peace)
- Elohim Chayim (He is the Living God)

There are just a few of His names. Check out the many blog articles, books and bible studies on this topic.

Why is knowing the different names of God, or at least some of them, (one website said there were 100 different names) so important for us?

Are you ready for this?

In every circumstance, every situation, God is there, wanting to show you a *new* side of Himself, a unique trait. Instead of focusing on the issue, the drama, the trauma, worrying about what you cannot control, focus on Him and ask Him, "Who are You for me right now that You haven't been for me before? What am I to learn in this? How am I to see You?"

For example, if you need healing, He is Jehovah Rapha. If you need stability in a chaotic time, He is your Tower of Refuge and Strength; He is your rock. If you feel chaos and confusion all around you and inside you, He is your Peace, Jehovah Shalom. See why it's important to know His Names, to have a list for you to reference?

Grab a journal and take some notes.

Answer these questions:

Who is God for you right now? Who has He been for you in the past?

What characteristics of God stand out to you the most right now?

Research the names of God and their meanings. Which ones jump out at you? Which ones resonate with you the most?

What themes are you seeing? What patterns? Write a description of God in your journal based on the answers above.

Chapter Nineteen

Time to Stop Running from Love

Stop running.

Do you think I don't know you are avoiding Me?

Do you think I can't tell when you are going through the motions or worship but don't really want an encounter with My Glory?

I know all things. I see the hidden places in your heart, the secret closets where guilt and shame have hidden your regrets, your fears, your anxieties. I see the basement of your soul, the cells in the dungeons where broken parts of you have been imprisoned and abused. I see the rooms of chaos and confusion, where the clutter hides your disorganized ways and patterns of hopelessness and oppression. You think you need to wear a mask of perfection to please everyone around you, yet I see the real you.

I see all of you. Every broken, hurting part who has tried to hold it together, yet failed time and time again. I see every part of you and love ALL of you. There is nothing I don't know about you. I indeed know you better than you know yourself. I know the family lines, the generational things passed along from father to child, mother to infant for centuries. I know, My child, I know.

I know your struggles, your battles, your heart's cry.

I see you. I hear you. I know you.

And I still love you. You cannot outrun My love.

I pursue you relentlessly, like a hound dog after a raccoon. The chase is on. You cannot escape My love. No matter how far you go, I am there. No matter how long you avoid Me, I am waiting. No matter how long you play the shell game, I will always know which shell you are under.

Just rest. Just stop and rest. Allow Me to come in. Give Me a tour of your heart and trust Me to bring healing, love and peace.

Won't you let Me in?

The presence of love.

Love that has no end.

Love that fills every gap, every hole, every crack.

Love that oozes into the wounds of your heart and soul.

Love that is tangible.

A love that covers you so well, you finally know you are truly accepted just as you are, really chosen to be part of the family. Regardless of what you have done, what you have seen, what happened to you, you are loved and wanted.

A love declaring you are of great worth and value.

You are loved with that kind of love, loved by the Most High King.

You have a Father who simply wants you to abide in His Presence, to sit in His lap, rest your head on His chest, listen to His heartbeat, a steady rhythm of love, joy and peace.

A love that says no more standing on the outside looking in, no more feelings of being neglected, unwanted, abandoned, unworthy.

You are no longer defined by actions, labels, the trauma of anything any man does or says.

The Most High King declares you are a much-loved child of God.

Why are you so scared of stepping into your identity, who I designed you to be? Why do you hesitate to fully charge after your destiny? Why do you second guess the words I have given to you? Why do you struggle with unbelief?

Do you not see I am good?

Do you not know I am for you?

Do you not realize I am always with you, ready to support, help and equip you for the task at hand?

Open the gate of your heart, open the door of your mind, open the window of your soul. Let Me in. I see those roots of insecurity, unbelief, fear of failure, fear of man, fear of success. I am coming to you, inside you to help you tear down walls, strongholds, platforms that do not serve Me. They've hidden your tormentors, attackers and guardians of evil.

I'm demolishing anything hindering My will being accomplished in your life. A glory hurricane is brewing and on track to strike your heart, your soul. My winds and rains of glory will storm through your realm. Anything not of My Kingdom will be washed away, obliterated by the raging winds I am sending.

It is time, beloved. It is time to embrace the fullness of who you are, who I created you to be. No more hiding, no more standing in the shadows, afraid of being noticed or seen. I am removing the cloak of invisibility you've worn for years.

It is time for you to emerge from your crystallis, flutter beautifully around My creation. You have pollinating to do, My beautiful butterfly. You have flowers, blossoms, plants to visit and work to do, so the fertilization, the pollination of My plants, My children, happens. Gifts, talents, projects, innovations, businesses, will be formed from your fluttering around these plants, these people.

As you worship, as you praise Me, the defilement of your land is being cleansed. Your praises and shouts reverse the curses and iniquity that's permeated the ground. Those before you walked in evil, iniquity, transgressions, corrupting the land, bringing chaos and confusion. The dark one knew the purpose and calling I placed on this ground, this city, this county, this country long ago. The frequency of your praises and worship shifts the atmosphere and moves mountains.

The rocks and trees have cried out for My Sons and Daughters to arise, for even they feel the defilement of the land, the corruption, the devastation of unchecked evil. My Blood covers, cleanses and redeems. As you worship Me, My blood pours upon your land, washing, flooding, and redeeming. A volcano of love erupts in the center, lava flows across the land, seeping into the soil underneath the surface.

Chapter Twenty

Idolatry vs. Adultery

Idolatry is adultery with other gods. Just as much of their temple worship includes sexual actions, the spiritual realm emulates the same. As you might already know, sexual intercourse establishes sexual covenants, soul ties. If idolatry provokes God's glory to lift from the gates of our land, then repentance from idolatry can open these gates for His glory to be restored.

Have you repented of putting other gods, any god, before your Lord? Have you taken the time to sit before Him and truly confess when you've put work, family, self, church, ball games, anything ahead of Him in your life? When you knew you needed to stop and do what He told you to do but you didn't have time because you had somewhere else to go? When you prioritize watching the latest and greatest show on Prime Video or the playoffs of your favorite team over spending time with Him.

Take time now to ask Holy Spirit what you need to apologize for, repent of and then do so. Need help forming the words? Pop back to the **Appendix** and choose a prayer.

Set me as a seal upon your heart,

As a seal upon your arm;

For love is as strong as death,

Jealousy as cruel as the grave;

Its flames are flames of fire,

A most vehement flame.

Song of Songs 6:8 NKJV

As I mentioned in the Names of God section earlier, one of His names is El Kanna, Jealous God. He adamantly tells us in the Ten Commandments to have no other gods before Him. Today, we barely realize the significance of idolatry and how it impacted the Israelites back in ancient times. Why did El Kanna tell the Hebrews to remain pure and not to intermingle with the other tribes? Why was it so important to avoid mixing cultures back then?

Michael Heiser talks about this in *Unseen Realm*. Others teach on the Elohim as well. Let me give a quick snapshot here to set the playing field for us. There was a Divine Council in those days, the Lord of Lords and the other gods. Each small god was given a nation to rule, Yahweh took Abraham's tribes for Himself.

Remember how the Philistines captured the ark of covenant in battle at Ebenezer and placed it in the temple of Dagon, their fish-man god, in Ashdod? Dagon fell on his face before the ark the next morning. The people of Ashdod uprighted their idol and put him back in his place. The next morning, the same thing happened, only this time his head and hands had broken off and were lying in the temple's doorway. Then a plague of tumors struck the people. Quickly assessing it was a curse from Yahweh, they moved it out of town and onto Gath. Much havoc and discord ensued until they finally convinced the Philistine rulers to return the ark back to Israel. (Did you know they also sent 5 gold tumors and 5 gold rats with the ark as a guilt offering?)

OK, sorry, I was bunny-trailing down bunny holes in 1 Samuel 5 and 6 and having a grand ole time. You should try it sometime. It's great fun.

Let's dive deeper on these 70 gods and nations. Jeffrey Kranz explains on his "Tower of Babel" post:

Moses tells the Israelites not to worship the sun, moon, the stars, and all the heavenly host like the other nations do. However, he tells the

Israelites that Israel's God *allotted these objects of worship* to the other nations. All the other nations of the world worship their gods, but Israel's God specifically made Israel his own portion (Deuteronomy 4:19–20). Later, Moses reminds the people that long beforehand, the Lord divided up the nations. And when he did so, he gave each of the nations their own lands and inheritances—but chose Israel for himself (Deuteronomy 32:7–9)

The people of ancient Israel believed they worshiped the chief God of all creation: the "Lord Most High." The other nations worshiped other gods, but Israel believed their God outranked any other deity.

We have several examples of this mentality showing up in the Old Testament. The Philistine idol Dagon cannot stand before the ark of the covenant (1 Samuel 5:1–5). A "prince of Persia" prevents a divine messenger from delivering an answer to Daniel's prayers (Daniel 10:12–13).

But the chief example of this is when God rescues Israel from slavery in Egypt. God famously brings ten plagues on the Egyptians, compelling the Pharaoh to release the Hebrews. However, these judgments aren't just on the oppressive Egyptian humans. The author of Exodus believes that Israel's God was exacting judgment on all the gods of Egypt, too (Exodus 12:12).

The gods of Egypt oppressed the Israelites. But they weren't the only gods who developed oppressive empires. Eventually, the Lord Most High said He's had enough.

The psalmist in Psalms 82 envisioned a heavenly courtroom, wherein Israel's God chastised the gods of the other nations. God told the other divine beings that they had been aiding the wicked and unjust people of the world, rather than leading the way Israel's God wanted them to: by protecting and defending the poor and the weak. Because of this, God would bring them all down, and disinherit them of the nations. At this point, the psalmist believed that not only was Israel God's portion (which was what Moses said), but all the nations were God's inheritance.[1]

Brian Godawa has a very interesting historical fiction series, starting with *Noah Primeval*, which begins the *Chronicles of the Nephilim*. Brian takes the supernatural background of the ancient lands and their gods, bringing them to printed form and your imagination. I love a good book based on biblical history brought to life, allowing you to picture and imagine how the bible story actually went down in everyday life.

Anyhow, Brian also has deep explanations at the end of each book with references and teachings on the fiction story. I highly recommend the series and the deep dive into Enoch, nephilim and the Watchers.

When you realize these beings truly exist and they are part of the gang that fell from heaven with Lucifer, your eyes open to the reality of the spiritual realm. We are spirit beings in a physical body. Often, we hear voices in our hearts, our minds, and we need to discern the type of spirit it is. Not everything you hear in your mind is from you or from the Lord. Some are from angels, some are evil.

Back to idolatry and cleansing the gates. Major inner healing and deliverance is required here. We need to reclaim the seats of authority, annul pacts with darkness, renew covenant with Jesus. Break off any idolatry or iniquity from our generational bloodlines. We get to shut the generational gates of sabotage.

Wondered why you're struggling for breakthrough? Feeling stuck and haven't been able to figure out the missing link for you to see your promise manifest? This might be the key.

Start by cleansing your bloodline, renouncing vows, pacts and agreements with the enemy. Renounce any inner vow you made as a child because of trauma you'd endured. Seek tribe members and find people to walk with you on this journey of reconciliation. Check out Dan Duval's

---

1. https://overviewbible.com/tower-of-babel/

Bride Ministries, Elijah House and Arthur Burk's Sapphire Leadership Group for more teachings and prayers on this intention.

Chapter Twenty-One

Temples of God

We sing, "Let our praises fill this temple."

Now, beloved, let me remind you, your body is the temple of God.

Let me repeat that for the ones in the back.

Let our praises fill this temple. Your body is the temple of God.

Grab that cup of coffee and let's ponder this together.

What do our praises filling the temple of God, our bodies look like? What if the words of the lyrics you sing are exactly what your heart, your mind need for restoration? What if they're what you require for full healing of your body and soul? When we sing along with the radio, whatever station you're listening to, whatever playlist you're streaming, what impact do those words, those beats and notes have on ourselves?

Fast food. Processed food. Cookies. Soda. Tacos. Potato chips. Unhealthy stuff. The foods that put us to sleep, inhibit clarity of mind, give us brain fog, dilutes our creativity and innovation. Adds pounds to our body. Do you realize fat is stored energy? We have resources stored our lifestyles don't require. We end up sick and tired of being sick and tired, suffering from cardiac issues, blood sugar issues, cancer, and so on.

We feed our minds and souls with junk food known as TV, radio, Netflix, Hulu, Firestick, movies, videogames, books that bring in corruption, contamination, destruction of brain cells, an apathy to the pain and suffering of others, foul language and violence.

We should study His Word, cultivate time with Him and being in His presence. Taking a prayer walk and spend time talking with Him, joining others for meals and times of sharing life. Singing, playing music, dancing, worshiping the Lamb of God.

What if our healing will manifest when we focus on worshiping Him more 24/7 and not just living the normal life with taking the kids to ball practice, working late to finish the project, binge watching the latest favorite show?

As His presence fills the temple, anything *not* of Him has to leave. If you need healing, worship Him more. I'm serious. I have heard many testimonies of people being healed during worship, not because someone came over and laid hands on them and prayed for them. They sang and shouted unto the Lord. Guess what happened. Jesus healed them without needing a person to do it.

It is time to learn to worship with our whole heart, with our bodies. To approach the Mercy Seat of God, the Throne Room, as confident sons and daughters of the Living God, ready to show our adoration, our awe, our amazement at who He is. Do not be content with the shadowy side of the veil. Let's get lost in His Presence. Soak in His love. When you surrender control of your life, your situations, your crisis, you let go and let God, then you have made room for Him to show up. You can step into rest and relax in Him.

Our praise is a weapon. Our shout shakes mountains. Our dance changes things. Abstaining from expressive worship hinders our relationship with God. Stop judging others' expressions of worship and focus on your own response to His Glory. Do not let your emotions determine how you worship. Let your worship impact your emotions and your thoughts.

He is worthy.

There is a reason we are told to fast and pray. There is a reason Jesus said He is the vine and we are the branches. We all need seasons of:

- Cleansing, detoxing, purging, pruning, trimming, refining
- Physically, spiritually, mentally, emotionally

If you detox, you fast certain things (aka diet). You should also look to fast things mentally and emotionally to remove toxins from your system. Purge those impediments from your mind. Cleaning out your mind is crucial for winning the battle of your mind. Uprooting of weeds such as:

- Bitterness
- Competition
- Rage
- Gossip
- Doubt
- Fear
- Strife
- Self-absorption
- Self-centeredness
- Judgmental
- Critical nature
- Negativity
- Self-martyr
- Lust

- Greed
- Gluttony
- Pride
- Slothfulness
- Fear of lack
- Need for acceptance of others
- Need for attention
- Performance mindset
- Religious mindset
- False humility
- Timidity
- Despair
- Discouragement
- Disappointment

Make a pile of these weeds to be burnt in a fire offering to God, a pleasing aroma in heaven. Plant seeds of:

- Love
- Joy
- Peace
- Patience
- Kindness
- Goodness

- Gentleness
- Faithfulness
- Hope
- Self-control
- Boldness
- Encouragement
- Purity
- Holiness
- Righteousness
- Beauty
- Strength
- Courage
- Humility

What walls are you ready and willing to tear down, to allow Jesus to demolish? What strongholds do you have that need to be destructed? What barriers to intimacy, connection, community do you have that need to be destroyed?

All of it is hindering your ability to climb higher on the glory mountain, to draw closer to Yahweh. That self-protective wall you built because you discovered at a young age people weren't to be trusted needs to come down. That tough guy exterior has to go.

Listen to the Father's heart about your walls.

Dear child, I desire all of you. Every 2000th part. I want to clear out any unwanted dead branches to make room for fruit-bearing branches. No twigs. My sweet child, we have a long intense journey ahead. I simply want you in the best form possible. You must train spiritually, mentally, physically and emotionally for the battles ahead.

Chapter Twenty-Two

All About Commitment

Musicians perform on stage before gatherings of My sheep. My church sings of My Presence, their surrender to Me, their wish to serve, to worship, to come deeper. Yet, when the time comes to act out those lyrics, they forget what they sang. They love My Presence, My Glory, My Love in the moment, in the sanctuary. But when it's time to work, to lead, to guide, to operate their ministry, their company, they no longer want to serve or surrender. They forget in whose image they were created.

I desire a generation who will abide in My Presence. Who seek My Face in each moment, every day. Who I can lead with My eyes because of their focus on Me. They fixed their gazes upon My Face so they see My eyes move, they notice what I am looking at and respond accordingly. They observe the expressions of My eyes before I even speak a word and start to move immediately. They are ones who have sacrificed it all for the sake of the call. Ones who have surrendered completely.

I have had enough of whitewashed tombs pretending to be My shepherds. No more controlling, no more pride, no more criticism, no more religion, no more abuse. No more treating My children like slaves. I am raising up a generation of Moses'es to lead My people out of slavery, to bring them out of Egypt. Regardless of who Pharaoh is, I will bring forth a Moses to liberate the captives.

I am done dealing with a contaminated vessel, a corrupted form. I am pulling My chosen ones from the fire. Ones who have been purged, fired, pruned, processed to be ready to do My work. I am revealing them to the world in this season.

He is looking for a relational community led by a team. Examine Acts 2:46-47 NLT.

They worshiped together at the Temple each day, met in homes for the Lord's Supper, and shared their meals with great joy and generosity, all the while praising God and enjoying the goodwill of all the people. And each day the Lord added to their fellowship those who were being saved.

All the believers gathered daily in the temple, shared their meals together and exuded joy and generosity. They had a simplicity of heart. Praising God and having favor with ALL people.

They were *in* the world and influencing it for *good*.

It is time to catch the vision of God and anchor ourselves securely in Him.

It's not about quantity, the number of bodies in seats on a Sunday morning. It's not about being a megachurch, full of hypocrites, religion, indifference, apathy and laziness.

It's about quality. It's about a gathering of hungry followers of Christ who love Him and each other. They abide in His presence always, pressing in for more of Him. These warriors walk in His footsteps, advancing Kingdom with each step, taking His love to the world. They train together for battle before entering the war zone, ready to take the city for His domain.

Are you one of them? Pray this with me then.

Prayer:

May the fruit others eat from me this week be the Fruit of the Spirit, not fruits of bitterness, irritation, confusion, envy, jealousy, anger, judgment, criticism. May my walk be one that advances Your Kingdom with each step, each day. May I bring unity and alignment into the equation, the moment. May I walk in commitment and loyalty, showing up when required and trustworthy. Make me a servant who knows her identity as a much-loved child of God.

Chapter Twenty-Three

Letting Go of Self-preservation

Why are we shocked when others disagree with us, don't understand us, ridicule us, mock us or persecute us? Why do we strive for the approval and acceptance of man? Why do we worry about stupid stuff?

As we walk with the Lord, as we shine for Him, we must realize there are those who will hate the light, who will dislike us because of the Jesus they sense in us. Whatever their reasoning is, they don't like us. Our presence agitates them. Our words disrupt their disillusions. Our actions confuse them.

We are to be tenderhearted, not hardhearted like Pharaoh and others who turned their backs on God. We are not to be proud or arrogant but easily moved to love, compassion, sorrow by others. We are to be impressionable, devoted to Him, and affectionate. Not protected by walls of self-preservation.

Soak for a moment in this word from the Father.

Breathe in My Love.

Let My Peace Transcend.

Soak in My Glory.

Rest in My embrace.

Let Me fill you with My Joy.

Take your seat with Me. You've been told you are seated in heavenly places with Christ. Sit with Me.

Now is the time to take off the masks you thought you had to wear to fit in, to be accepted, to win approval, to be loved. Now is the time to examine what labels the enemy, the world, your family, yourself have given you over the years and review them with Me.

What have you been told you are? What lies are you believing instead of believing My Truth about you? What word curses have been spoken over you that you accepted and adopted? Where is the rotten apple, the moldy piece of cheese, the nasty leftovers you wouldn't even feed to the dogs? Yet it is there, inside of your heart, spreading toxins. What labels do you have that I did not give to you?

Make a list. Detail them all because I want to respond to every single one of them. And tell you how I see you, how I made you instead. To remove all of those labels and replace them with divine identity statements. Inheritance words. It is time to move out of Egypt. Your deliverer has come. Liberation Day is here. You are being emancipated. You are no longer a slave. I have called to be Mine, chosen you to be My much-loved child.

Do not settle for life in Babylon. Do not acquiesce to the way things have always been. Do not tolerate good enough.

I am calling you out to rebuild My temple in My city. To leave the world's city, the world's ways and abide in the land I gave to your ancestors, to redig the wells of revival, to rekindle the glory fires, to release the RUACH breath of God into a dry abandoned land. Watch what I will do when you step out in faith.

Self-Reflection Time

What are the areas you refuse to allow Jesus in? What rooms in the house known as your life have you locked the doors and chosen to not allow Him in? The ones that are closed to visitors? What fleshly spots are you refusing to crucify?

These all point to idols, to areas where your love for the Lord is not currently greater than your commitment to that idol.

Name it what it is. Stop denying. Stop pretending everything is okay and fine. Remember the scientific method. First, you must identify the problem in order to develop a viable solution and activate upon it. The Church needs to stop wearing masks and putting on airs. It's time to confess, repent and turn from our wicked ways. It's time to put it all on the altar and sacrifice it.

> "If we walk in the spirit daily, we will not fulfill the lusts of the flesh." ~ Rich Harris

We must choose to walk in the spirit each day. This means we need to ask the following questions, answering truthfully.

- What parts of your mind, your soul is still in bondage?
- Where are you not walking in abundance, in victory?
- What lies are you believing about yourself, others, the Lord, the world?

Find out the answers to these questions and then ask Holy Spirit what the TRUTH is. Ask for help to break free of the old belief systems and lies, help to embrace freedom.

If you realized the impact your whiney, crybaby ways had on your life, your health and attitude, on your family, you'd cringe, maybe even fall over in a faint. If you truly knew how living in fear and anxiety affected your physical and mental health, you'd stab it in the steely heart with your sword in a New York minute.

But you don't. You don't see how fear is at the root of your allergies. You don't fathom how anxiety over stupid stuff is hindering your body's ability to heal itself, fostering a lovely environment for cancer and other nastiness to grow. The hormones are released into your blood stream due to overstress. The self-sabotage, self-loathing you have attack your immune system.

This, beloved, is why it is so crucial to peel back the layers of the onion called your heart and deal with the wounds, to let Jesus in.

It's storytime. Grab your milk and cookies. Ready? Here we go:

One day I was having a pity party and feeling a bit persnickety. Alright, I was fussing about my life and current circumstances. Then, Audacious One told me:

Quit sniveling. Seriously. Enough already. I have heard enough. Are you Mine? Are you My sunbeam? Are you strong and courageous? Are you ready for battle and to win the victory for Me? You simply must fight. The battle victory is already yours, if you but fight.

Well then. Allow me to take my seat, shut my mouth and just listen, Lord.

We are in training for gaining ground. My husband did a full Ironman triathlon in 2017. I quickly learned, when you are training for an Ironman triathlon, you're ready for a 5K, 10K or 2o-mile bike ride any day of the week without having to train or prepare. You're conditioned and ready to go. Your standard level of fitness is higher than average, better than normal. Just before race day, you're doing century-mile rides and running 20+ miles on training days. The idea of stepping up to the starting line for a sprint triathlon or a 10K race doesn't make you blink your eyes because you could do that in your sleep. You've been on this training journey for months, even years, now and a six-mile run is considered child's play compared to the long run you have on your schedule for this weekend.

Let's take that analogy into the spiritual world. When you fast, you can start with skipping one meal. No, sir, you don't need to jump into fasting with a strict 40-day water fast. We have a gracious God, not a tyrant. Skip one meal, then two. Do a juice fast for a day or two. Skip a meal and drink juice or a protein shake instead. I prefer juice fasts or Daniel fasts (fruits and veggies) because I'm still getting some calories and nutrition to help me continue working. One day I'll do a water fast. Maybe even for a few days. As I just said, work up to these things. Once you're fasting regularly, the idea of skipping a meal isn't a big deal because you've conditioned your flesh, you've established authority and self-control. The neural pathways have been traced already.

Now let's talk about studying, morning devotions, ending your day with Him. Years ago, I heard about getting up early to spend time with Jesus every time I turned around. I heard the testimonies and delight of those who were early birds and sought the Lord by sunrise. *Sigh*. Each time I spent the night at my grandmother's house as a child, I would find her on the recliner with her bible in the morning, communing with her Jesus. My brother, my husband, and I all have been at my parents' house in the morning and seen my mom in her recliner, feet and bible up. On a recent visit, I was sitting in the living room with her and she read Isaiah to me as I drank coffee and did my own reading.

I used to journal prayers in the morning before I even crawled out of bed. Nope, not getting out of bed yet, but I'll talk to Jesus from here. Thanks.

Then I started reading the Bible and journaling. Eventually I ended up converting a storage closet upstairs to a prayer closet (Thanks *War Room* for the idea.) and had my little bookcase, blankets and corkboard set up for business. Each morning, my honey + apple cider vinegar water and I ventured into the prayer room to meet with Papa. Often, the cat, Harvey, and/or my brown dog, Davi, had to join us.

Harvey spent lots of time with Jesus in those days. He was a rescue kitty and required lots of TLC for months until he felt safe and loved. Until he would snuggle close and purr. I would bring him in the closet with me and he'd hide behind the corkboard. Now he tends to sit on my desk, trying to walk across the keyboard as I work.

Years later, I naturally wake up and spend an hour with the Lord. Reading, studying, journaling, listening to worship music. Depends on what I feel led to do that day. Even if you only have five minutes, start with five.

Or spend the last minutes of the day with Him before falling asleep. Get your mind right before dreamtime.

Even five minutes of focused attention on the Lord per day will make a difference. I even bet you'll see time multiplied supernaturally, so you find you end up with more five-minute segments to spend with Jesus.

Chapter Twenty-Four

Words

Be careful of the words you speak.

Make them soft and sweet.

You may have to eat them one day.

Too many people are complaining and whining their way through life. Think about it. Who in your circle of friends tends to be constantly grumbling, growling, griping about someone, something, somewhere? Do you have a family member who is Negative Nancy, always complaining, fussing, caterwauling about one thing or another?

Whining never changed the world. It is high time we stopped justifying our fears and started doing something with the gifts and talents we've been given. Stop coddling each other. We need to grab ahold of the man we're wrestling with and ask for a blessing.

Paul tells us to give thanks in all things. To pray unceasingly. Ever wonder *why* he said to do that? Forget about the what or how of praying unceasingly for a moment. There have been many books written, sermons preached on that. Instead, let's focus on the why. Why on earth would he tell us to give thanks 24/7/365?

Ever think maybe, just maybe, giving thanks amid every situation, every moment is a way of conducting warfare? It is a tactic used by warriors to shift atmospheres and push through walls. Maybe our thanksgiving affects activities in the heavens in ways we don't yet fathom. Maybe when we choose to give thanks instead of complaining, we shift things. We put another piece in the bowls in heavens, just waiting for them to tip over.

Back to the fussing, the caterwauling. How much authority are you giving to fear, pride and anxiety? Are you speaking out about your fears, your insecurities, your anxious thoughts? Are you giving them voice and releasing them into the air? Do you know what Isaiah 55:11 says?

Words manifest into real life. You have the power of life and death in your tongue. Don't believe me? Think about Creation: God spoke, and it came into existence. The same creative power is within you. If you have been filled with the Holy Spirit, then you have the Resurrection Power inside of you.

It's time we started walking in the power He's given us. Will Hart said it best, "You're going to scare the townfolk when you walk in the power and authority." Speak life over your dreams, your families, your businesses. Speak goodness and mercy over your city, your state, your nation. Speak good health and wellness over your mind, body, soul, even your finances.

Do you realize what being royalty means? To be a queen in the court means you speak in the name of the King. You can reverse every curse as you come into true power and anointing.

You are the sound engineer of your own life. Do a sound check. Review the live microphones and the volume of each one. Determine who is currently speaking into your life, your situation and decide if they should have their mic cut off or amplified. Check for harmony and balance in the sounds you hear. Does it all fit together and come into alignment with the Word of God? Does it bring life and abundance or death and destruction? If it doesn't, you know it is not of the Lord. Cut the words off and toss them at the feet of Jesus.

Vanquish all the inner voices distracting you from the still small voice of wisdom. Cut their mics off. Ask Holy Spirit to guide you in how to silence the inner critics. Ask Him to show you their source, their open door to your heart so you can close it. Seek the wise counsel of a Spirit-filled friend or leader to walk you through inner healing to get the chaos in your mind to turn into a peaceful, serene abode.

You can't be optimistic and faith-filled unless you own your words. Apologize when you get off-course and say things you know were out of line, were cruel and crude, were demeaning and disrespectful. Practice speaking kindly and edify others regularly. You're retraining your mouth to speak new ways, new things, new patterns. You might be used to complaining, cursing, caterwauling. None of that is allowed anymore. You are not an alley cat.

Instead, you now get to bless others, yourself and your surroundings. You get to speak *life*. Imagine a bunch of believers running around your town, blessing the grocery store clerk, saying thank you and doubling the tip for their waitress, greeting people in any place of business with a smile. What if you took a deep breath and choose to exude grace and patience when the computer isn't cooperating with the service representative you're dealing?

I was just telling a friend I needed to ask the Lord if He thought I had enough patience yet. I have been hearing service techs thank me for being patient for years. Computers lock up, take extra time to load, and so on. The bane of technology.

As I reflected on the question of having enough patience, the Holy Spirit whispered, "Maybe it's not about patience. What if I simply want you to show grace and compassion to a group of workers who typically get yelled at, berated and growled at as part of their jobs? What if your assignment is to brighten their day and make them smile for a change? To shine My light."

We recently bought a new oven range for the kitchen. The oven didn't work upon the arrival of the new machine. I called for servicing, so they sent out a technician. It needed a new ignitor. On the third tech visit and second shipped part, I just laughed when the repairman told me the part was broken and he had to order another one. He was amazed and grateful I was not angry and wasn't yelling at him about a brand-new oven that didn't work. It wasn't his fault; there was no reason to take it out on him or be angry with him.

Let's just say after three months and four repairman visits, I called the manufacturer and asked for help. The woman on the repair service line heard my story. "Oh no, let me get you over to another department so they can process the replacement range for you. Enough of this already. You've waited long enough." I could have cried at that moment. *Finally, someone is going to send me a stove with an oven that works.* My patience amazed the service rep who answered the transferred call; she wouldn't have waited as long to order a replacement stove. I was trying to not just toss out something that was still good but wanted to repair it first.

Then the delivery man informed me I had made the right decision; if it had issues coming off the assembly line, it didn't bode well for future functionality.

I've learned to just wait, be patient and it'll restart, reboot, reset.

This also applies to our own transformation and others. Sometimes we need to realize God is still working on us, on our family members and our colleagues. We need to extend grace, patience and mercy instead of growling and grumbling because the process hasn't finished yet. Our words have impact and we want to make sure it is the impact we desire.

Chapter Twenty-Five

Speak the Opposite

Thank God for your struggles, your trials. Thank Him for even the bad choices you made. Let go of the ideal, the expectations you had. Lay them at the foot of the Cross.

Stop looking at me cockeyed, like I am being ridiculous. Paul tells us in 1 Thessalonians 5:18 to give thanks in *ALL* things. Guess what that word ALL means there. ALL. Not just the fun things. Not the cool things. Not just the pleasant things. Not just the ones you asked for or wanted. But *all* things.

If you are humble, if you are willing, if you surrender your will and life to Him, He will work it all out for good. He knew you'd make that decision, choose that partner, walk through the door, and He planned a way to rescue you, to weave into the tapestry of your life and make something beautiful of it.

Now, let's get back to thanksgiving. Step out of your current problem, circumstance, situation. Shift your focus from it for a moment.

Sit with me for a minute, grab yourself a cup of coffee or hot tea. Got your mug? OK, take a sip and listen to me now.

Your current trial and tribulation are not about YOU.

OK, I'm giving you a minute to collect yourself. I can see you're lambasted by this epiphany. Ready to hear more? Here we go. Whatever it is that you're enduring, suffering through, persevering through right now is about several things.

1. Drawing you closer to HIM. In the middle of the storm is when we hit our knees in the middle of the boat, "JESUS, I need you. LORD, where are You? Don't you see I'm about to drown? Please, Lord, save me...." We realize we *need* Him when we're in over our heads, when we can't touch the ground underneath the water anymore, when we're overwhelmed. We tend to get puffed up and think we can handle life on our own when everything is hunkydory. When everything starts going sideways, then, "Oh hello, uh, Lord, I know I haven't reached out in a while, but could you....."

2. Our trials and tribulations, what we have survived are the areas where we have jurisdiction, we have authority to help others, to support others, to bring them to their own victory. Case in point, I have dealt with hostile work environments and had to learn to walk in peace and put on my spiritual armor before meetings very quickly. If you are in a similar situation, I can encourage and empower you to walk from victory in your workplace. I know the torment and oppression that can exist in an office and strategies to deal with it, conquer it, shift atmospheres. Been there, done that, got the t-shirt. I can encourage and coach others in similar situations.

3. He wants to teach us a new language, the language of His Kingdom. To speak life and not death. Regardless of the situation, we need to control our words and not release curses or death. We need to learn to put a muzzle on it when we can't get a grip on our tongue.

My mom challenged us as young'uns, "If you can't say anything nice, don't say anything at all." Our other challenge was if she caught my brother and me saying something mean and nasty to each other, we then had to say two nice things about the other one. Telling my brother he had an outstanding sister didn't count as one of my compliments, either. I can't fathom why either; can you?

Methinks my mom knew we were in a war and words were weapons even then.

Which side have you been fighting on lately? God's or the Accuser's? Too many Christians have been working on the side of the Accuser for too long. Gossip, fear-mongering, judging, criticizing, harassing, biting remarks. We act little different than the people in *The Scarlet Letter* by Nathaniel Hawthorne. Mind you, it was published in 1850 and set in the Puritan Massachusetts the previous century, yet we still can act the same today. Assessing others' sins and condemning them to wear a scarlet letter to state what their sin is. We pick up our stones with the Pharisees, ready to execute punishment upon the guilty, when Jesus tells us, "He who hasn't sinned can cast the first stone."

"Weight in Gold" by JJ Heller is playing on the Fresh Christian playlist on Amazon Music right now. JJ explains in her song how words are worth their weight in gold.

The power of life and death are in the tongue. Are you speaking forth life or death in your daily conversations?

Chapter Twenty-Six

Testify

Somebody testify. Ever listen to some old-school gospel music or preaching? I guarantee you heard that line. Yet I wonder how many of us ever contemplated the actual definition of the word testify.

Do you know the meaning of the word "testify"? Do you really?

You might gripe, complain, fuss, whine, grumble, grouch, gossip, criticize regularly. But do you ever testify of the goodness of God? Testify of His mercy, His love, His steadfast ways? His provision for you? His protection, His guidance, His majesty, His glory, His power? His grace, His joy, His strength, His healing, His miracles? Do you testify about your God more than you talk about anything else? More than you judge, more than you antagonize others, more than those snarky, sarcastic remarks you're known for?

Let's check out Merriam-Webster's definition of testify.

> 1: to make a solemn declaration under oath for the purpose of establishing a fact (as in a court). 2a: to make a statement based on personal knowledge or belief : bear witness. b: to serve as evidence or proof. 3: to express a personal conviction. transitive verb. 1a: to bear witness to : ATTEST. b: to serve as evidence of : PROVE. 2: to de-

clare under oath before a tribunal or officially constituted public body.

Do you realize testifying leads to overcoming?

> ***11*** *And they overcame him by the blood of the Lamb and by the word of their testimony, and they did not love their lives to the death. Revelation 12:11 NKJV*

I know you have read that verse, heard that verse before. But, grab that dissecting knife you used in High School Biology and come with me into the Science Laboratory for a moment.

No, no sitting on the other side of the room with the microscopes, thinking you are now a microbiologist. Focus!

Here, sit with me on this stool. OK, we got the squirmy verse in the pan. You pin it down and I'll start cutting. Or did you want to begin the dissection?

Ready? I know, we're dealing with the Living Word of God; what did you expect?

First cut: They overcame by the blood of the Lamb. Who's the Lamb in this verse? The Lamb who was slain before the beginning of time, the Lion of Judah, the Messiah. The One who shed his blood on a cross so that we might be reconciled to the Godhead. His blood redeems us. Nothing else does. Not our own good works, our own bloodline, our own networks and gifts. Nothing but the blood of Jesus.

OK, take the scalpel and make another cut. Ah, the *word of their testimony.* Back to that testify verb again. Here we go. Your words are an uppercut to the jaw of the enemy. The heavens are shaken by your declarations of goodness, thanksgiving, provision and healing. Your decrees have a tangible effect on your world.

Think about it. You testify in a court of law to bear witness to what you saw, what you did or did not do. You swear to tell the whole truth, and nothing but the truth. What truth have you been testifying about in your chats with friends, your conversations with family, at your job? Are you glorifying God with your words or is the thought of Him listening to your conversations and reading your messages a bit unnerving?

Want to win some ongoing battles in your life? Watch your words.

One final cut on this verse: *and they did not love their lives to death.* Now what on earth are we talking about here? They didn't love their lives to death. First peek inside the cut, shows us martyrdom. Those who stood in the face of death, challenged to deny their Savior and chose to stand instead.

But, lean this way and look deeper. Look at the death to self, to the flesh piece you just sliced through. We are challenged to pick up our cross daily, to die to self, to deny flesh and follow Christ. To die to our own dreams, desires, our parents' dreams for our lives, our hopes for the future. To let go of control, as if we ever really had any anyways, and give it all to God. To say, "Here I am, Lord, send me," and then go wherever He leads. To surrender yourself on the altar, "Not my will, but Yours, Lord."

OK, go over to the lab sink and wash up. It's storytime now.

Years ago, I was at a Global Awakening conference in Pennsylvania. At one point in worship, I was laying across the stairs to the stage. No, I don't remember how I ended up sprawled over them but there I was. I saw myself on the altar, resembling Isaac with Abe that day long ago. I was surrendering to Him. The Father took a sword and killed my flesh self. Right then. Right there. Then He took my hand and raised me up in new life. The old is gone; the new has come.

I was no longer the same person. I was a new creation in Christ, never to be the same again.

As followers of Jesus, we are called to lay down our lives and follow Him. Give up the normal white picket fence life and chase after the Wild

Goose named Holy Spirit. We are to be mavericks, renegades, warriors, berserkers, even. Men and women willing to go where He leads, say what He says and do what He says to do. We have divorced fear of man and fear God instead. We have given up on trying to be average, normal or accepted within worldly circles. We accept the reality that life will never be the same.

In the poker game of life, we put it all on the table and shove it into the middle. "I'm all in and I call you," is our declaration to the Lord.

We love Jesus more than life itself.

Chapter Twenty-Seven

Being Intentional about Praise & Worship

When you attend a worship service, are you there to assess the performance, be entertained, judge the worship team, the preacher's sermon OR are you there to worship Yahweh?

What is your intent? Which is your focus?

I have heard complaints about all the above. I have even been the one complaining at times. Yet He arrested me one Sunday and asked me the above questions. "What do you want to do, My child?"

You make the choice. Either be intentional about your praise and worship, or the enemy can easily distract you. You can always find an imperfection with an imperfect vessel. What has your attention?

When we choose to be submitted to authority and leadership, when we choose to walk in honor and humility, not being afraid of man or controlled by man, just simply recognizing the order God has established and following it, we find blessing and grace abounds. We find completion and connection in ways we couldn't have imagined before. Lone ranger prophets who wear badges of isolation and are residents of the local orphanage will never understand what it means to be part of a tribe, to belong in a community of believers.

Yes, I know you've been hurt, abused, mistreated, ridiculed and berated by church leadership. I know because I had similar wounds too. Until I dealt with those wounds, chose to forgive the ones who hurt me, betrayed me, didn't see me, and released the bitterness, the judgments to Jesus so He could heal me, I couldn't step into the new season, the next thing God had for me. I couldn't connect to new leadership because I still expected them to act just like every leader before had acted. I just knew how the story would play out. Then I had to admit I was bitter, I was resentful, and I wasn't letting Jesus have His way in that area of my life.

So, I had to let go, I had to forgive, I had to realize harboring grudges wasn't harming the person I was angry with. It was hurting me. I had been in enough pain for long enough; it was time to deal with the roots once and for all.

No, sir, it wasn't easy. No, it wasn't fun. No, it wasn't a one-and-done thing or a quick, snap your fingers and it's over. It was a process. Honestly, I probably still have a few roots to go back and attack. It's like peeling layers back on an onion. There are a lot of them. But I can tell you how freeing and liberating doing so has been. It's a game-changer.

As you walk through dealing with your own issues, take time to listen to what others are saying. Focus and determine how you can help, how you can meet their needs. We are all selfish unless we do something about it. Be careful on how you talk to others. Treat others, including those in your own household, with honor and respect.

Chapter Twenty-Eight

Overcoming Fear

Quiet your mind. Stop the raging storm of negative thoughts. Cease the self-defeating, self-rejecting, self-loathing. Arrest any and all renegade thoughts.

Instead, listen, My child, simply listen to what Heaven is declaring over you. Hear what I am singing over you. Soak in what We are decreeing in your life. Listen to My voice alone. Focus solely on My words. Reset your mind. Blaze new neural pathways of joyful intentionality and thanksgiving. Retrain your brain.

Pray this aloud: *I open up my heart to You now, Lord. Do what only You can do. Have your way in me now.*

The Lord has given us His breath. He wants us to breathe life into our situations. Into the valley of dry bones in our lives. We shouldn't be waiting on Him to do it. He created the universe with His words, with His exhale. What are we speaking forth, creating with our own words? Let there be ____. His breath in us means we can decree a thing into existence. We should use His Word as our asthma inhaler. We breathe in the Word of God daily to cleanse our bodies, minds, and souls.

Just listen. No need to perform. No need to do. No need to speak. Just listen, My child.

You've been given the Mind of Christ. It is time to use it. Realize the door of opportunity has fear attached to it. Stop letting fear paralyze you.

Decide today you are moving forward regardless of what it looks like, regardless of who says what to you. Make your mind up you are focused on accomplishing the Work of the Lord that's been assigned to you.

Sometimes this means you must pick yourself up by the scruff of the neck and get moving.

Grab some milk and cookies, your favorite blankie and have a seat here on the floor with me. It's story time.

In the summer of 2020, I began battling horrible eye allergies. It seemed like anything and everything I'd been using for months, even years, suddenly didn't like me. I first thought it was a mixture of sweat and dust that had gotten into my eyes and all over my eyelids from a fence-building project I had been working on with my husband. After several weeks, we discovered it had turned into an eye infection. I can't tell you how many kinds of over-the-counter eye meds I tried during that season. The optometrist finally gave me an antibiotic with steroids to make it go away.

Then, I unsuspectingly would use the facial wash or shampoo I had been using for months and whammy. The allergies flared again. I went for months wearing glasses and no makeup because I felt awful. Most of the time, contacts or makeup would set off the allergies.

Obviously, I was asking lots of friends to pray for me over this trial. One eventually told me what I already knew to be true, the root of allergies was fear. The obvious question was: *What was I so afraid of?* I thought and thought, I prayed and prayed about this. Amid swollen eyelids, itchy eyes and feeling miserable anytime they flared, I sought the Lord, asking what I was missing. Where had fear taken up residence and I was in denial about it?

You see, I was the fearless kid, not scared of bugs, spiders, blood, guts, heights, even public speaking. (I was preaching in my little country church at eighteen years old as a certified lay preacher.) I was totally *not* a candidate for being on the old show *Fear Factor*. So, when I was battling allergies, something wasn't adding up for me.

Eventually, after lots of suffering, I started to connect dots. I joined a business networking group that month. I set up my new company's website that month. God had given me a business idea and I had moved forward with it. Little did I know then in my subconscious was a fear of failure and a fear of success. Yep, danged if I do, darned if I don't. I found a new friend in my allergist, who gave me a free of everything facial cleanser and lotion to try, just to be able to wash my face again.

Side bar: Who knew most makeup companies and skin care companies put *HORRIBLE* things in their products? Heavy metals, abrasive dyes and other yucky ingredients that have no business being in something we apply to our bodies. No wonder we react so negatively to these things.

Anyhow, we did the 30+- point test to find out what I was allergic to. Nothing really strongly responded the way my eyes did when I had an allergy flare. We had a few things to avoid as a result, but nothing concrete and solid to signify that we had discovered the root cause.

Meanwhile, I continued on my inner healing path, releasing things to God, asking Him to renew and redeem me. Asking Him to shine His light on me. One thing led to another, and I started discovering who I was again, remembering the truth of what I had accomplished so far in life. Realizing I had to rely on Holy Spirit to provide, to show up, to strategize for me to do what He asked me to do. To complete my tasks. That I needed to move when He said move, do what He said to do and nothing else. To stop trying to do things in my might and rely on His strength instead. And put on my construction boots with their steel toes and kick the hindparts of fear out the doors of my heart and soul.

> The enemy wants you to think he has the authority to actually do everything you fear. ~Justin Carpenter

A major piece to breakthrough here was listening to ones who love me. My husband, my parents, my mother-in-law, new friends who had strong relationships with the Lord and spoke truth, even when it sliced soul from spirit inside of me. They knew me, they saw me, they refused to sit back and let me stay in the analysis paralysis zone. They didn't agree with fear. They set the bar higher and told me to come up. They took a stance that said, "I love you too much to let you wallow in this pit. To allow you to give up on yourself, to let fear keep you from what you were created to do."

About nine months into the journey, I realized I had stopped using my eye drops every morning and night. I realized I was using different products and not reacting. I was able to wear makeup and use something other than the super free cleanser for once. The allergies were gone, and I didn't even realize it at first. When I went after the true spiritual root, I was victorious.

My friend, the one who did a lot of arm pulling and butt kicking over those months, told me once I had a window of opportunity to seize. Get it done or I would miss it. Stop making excuses, stop procrastinating, stop waiting for things to be perfect and just do it. It landed like a punch to the gut. I knew what she said was true. I didn't want to have to look Jesus in the eyes and know I messed up; I failed to complete my assignment because I was allowing fear to control me.

I made the decision to walk into my identity, to embrace who He created me to be, to fulfill what the books of destiny in Heaven say about me. Granted, I get tested on this again and again. For example, as I finalize this book, the allergies flared again. "OK, Lord, help me to uproot this fear."

Now, isn't it time for you to do the same? Choose today to step into grace, the goodness of God and divine abundance. Choose faith instead of fear, peace instead of anxiety and trust instead of worry. You must conquer fear to move forward. Be brave. Ask the Holy Spirit to help you discover the roots of your fears and to assist with yanking them out of the soil of your heart and soul so you can be free.

Walk in the knowledge of who you are. Embrace your identity. Accept yourself just as you are. The freckles, the flabby arms, the pointy elbows, the gray hair, the quirks, warts and scars. Accept it all. Choose to see yourself as I see you.

Change the station in your mind that has been telling you for decades that you are inadequate, incompetent, and an imposter. That you'll never change.

Stop listening to that podcast. Change the channel to Mine, the Identity Network. It streams live 24/7/365. When I tell you who you are in My eyes, how much I love you. How I created you and designed you for a specific purpose. You don't need walls and strongholds to protect you anymore. I am your shelter, refuge, your rearguard. I sent My Son to die on a cross so you could walk in complete freedom.

Isn't His sacrifice worth the cost of you walking out of the cage you've been in?

Here's an acrostic I discovered about taking every thought captive.

M – Mute the lies.

I – Invite the truth.

N – Know the difference.

D – Decide which to listen to.

Interrogate your fears. Recognize their origin. Ask them where they came from. Pay attention, because wherever thoughts from Satan are attacking us shows us where our greatest strengths are. Ask Papa to give you opposite thoughts. Reflect on the scripture: He gives us beauty for ashes, strength for fear, gladness for mourning, peace for despair.

Chapter Twenty-Nine

Tree of Knowledge of Good and Evil

The world seeks to understand every little thing. Intellect is valued to the point of idolatry. Eons later, we're still eating from the Tree of the Knowledge of Good and Evil. We are more obsessed with understanding circumstances, how things work, the logic of an action, how something happened instead of being obsessed with the love of God, obsessed with knowing Him and Him alone. Are we focused on comprehension of anything and everything or focused simply on the face of our Bridegroom, our Kinsman Redeemer?

He told us to seek His Kingdom first and all things would be added unto us. Maybe, just maybe as we seek after His Kingdom, solely focus on Him, His glory, His love, His righteousness, His justice and mercy, the Knowledge, the wisdom of heaven is imparted to us because knowing Him in intimate moments is more desired than knowing ways, plans and programs of man.

Maybe the fear of God grows within us as we get to know Him better. As we truly grasp who He is, really who He is, we stand in awe. We collapse to our knees in acknowledgement of royalty, of His presence. To know who created the heavens and earth and know He loves us is incomprehensible to the soul's intellect. It requires the spirit to come forward to wrap its mind around it. Mere education from worldly systems does not explain this in greater detail.

People chase after more degrees, more training, more education. Yet degrees of divinity, theology, graduate degrees from a divinity school do not mean a person has a clue who I am. It doesn't mean they have an intimate relationship with Me, Holy Spirit or Yeshua. More education is not always a better thing. Intimacy with Me is. Surrender to Me.

The humility and holiness of their walk speaks volumes. Education and experience matter not if their walk does not shine with My glory. Too many leaders, so-called leaders, have walked in pride, iniquity, sexual sins, control, under the power of leviathan. Unwilling to humble themselves before My throne. I have given them ample time to repent, to change. Many have chosen to continue on their left-handed paths. My day of reckoning is coming. The bowls of iniquity are close to spilling over. Brace yourselves. The coming bloodbath will be horrendous.

Most of My children now are of the generation of Joshua who entered the Promised Land. They've never seen war. They are not battle-worn, battle tested. I need strong mature sons and daughters to shepherd, to lead in these coming days. Ones who have wisdom and can remain centered in My shalom peace, regardless of what it looks like. What they see with their natural eyes. I need ones able to see with their spiritual eyes, hear with spiritual ears. To orchestrate what I need to have done, to equip their siblings for battle, to edify and then empower. I need ones ready to be sent on a moment's notice. Ones who hear My voice and draw close to Me. Ones who aren't scared of the fight, of a little blood.

Just as Levite priests slaughtered the sacrificial animals, these new priests will slaughter the sacrifice on My altars. It is time. You need to stay focused on the throne.

We are to abide in Him, to discover more and more about Him, His Kingdom, rather than worldly knowledge. Stay focused on Him.

The shaking has begun. Yahweh isn't standing for predators and hypocrites to be His representatives any longer. It's time to truly *know* God and not a false counterfeit.

Chapter Thirty

Way of Life

Do you enter the Throne Room with joy, love and such energy, you simply cheer and yell? You should. Can you imagine loving God more, knowing Him more? I can't, but I can't wait to do so.

Growing in faith is a constant process of daily renewing our trust in Jesus, of discovering more of His love for us, leading to loving Him and others more.

As we do so, we need to accept evidence of what God has done in our lives and in the lives of others. Jesus said that we will worship in Spirit and in Truth. Life is a blend of the written Word of God and the Living Word of God. We cannot get so caught up in trying to find something in scripture to prove a point, to make an argument, we lose track of whose we are and living a life that reflects Jesus.

Look at what they have invented in the last fifty years. Mobile phones, computers, and more. Shall we not use any technology to advance the Kingdom of Heaven because it wasn't in Scripture? Shall we not use electricity or drive vehicles because they weren't in the Bible?

Could it be that there is a new revelation being released to the children of God in this hour because of the times we are living in? That mysteries and treasures that were stored up centuries ago are now being revealed and discovered for such a time as this? Daniel and John were both told not to reveal what they had seen yet. Do you not think we're now in the times foretold?

What an exciting time to be alive.

Obviously, we shouldn't believe everything we see, hear or watch without judgment or assessment. We need to develop greater discernment in this hour to sort through what is good, pure and holy and what is corrupt, contaminated.

The Bride needs to realize her enemy takes the written word of God and twists it to his liking. He creates a counterfeit bill of the Word to trap and trip the unsuspecting, unknowing, untrained ear of believers. If you don't have an intimate relationship with the Lord, if you do not know the Voice of the Shepherd well enough to tell the difference between His voice and the voice of a wolf or hireling, it's high time you learned. Jesus said His sheep know His voice. We need to know when He is speaking to us and when it's not Him.

How do you know if a word is from the Lord? Glad you asked. Here are several keys to unlocking that door:

- Does it align with Scripture?
- Does it convict, instead of condemn?
- Does it bring life, instead of death?
- Does it bring peace to your spirit?
- Does it resonate deep within?
- Is it pure, holy and righteous?
- Does it agree with the knowledge that He is a good, good Father?
- Does it bring clarity or confusion?
- Is it enlightening?

You must be able to say yes to these questions to verify the message is from the Lord. He does not change and does not waver in His ways.

He is the great I AM. This is how you learn to tell the originator of the word you've received. Do not just accept any thought, any message, any prophetic word you receive. Judge it, weigh it on the divine scale. Does it balance with His Word? Does it align with His Plumbline?

We need to stop being so naive and ignorant. (The neighbor's donkey agrees; she just started braying.) Arrest your thoughts and check their passports, their papers. Where did they come from and where are they going? Put on your Dick Tracy hat and get to investigating those prophetic words you were given. Shine the light on them and ascertain their origin. Stop just accepting anything and everything said to you, every thought that pops into your head. *You* have the power to reject curses, judgments and lies. Isn't it time you started exercising that power?

Amid taking authority over our own minds and judging prophetic words we've received, we also need to review statements made to us, about us. Allow me to give you an example.

Years ago, during a walk through the valley of the shadow of death, a church leader joked that if the locals tried to kidnap me in a foreign country known for such crimes, the locals would quickly pay a ransom to return me instead. He also commented how being around me wore him out and he needed a nap afterwards.

He was being sarcastic and clowning around. I was oppressed, depressed and stressed in those days. I was not in the frame of mind where I was ready to handle such a verbal assault from a pastor. He apologized after I told him how he had hurt my feelings. I had to forgive and let go of those words, to cut them off so they would not continue to have a negative impact on me, making me feel unwanted and like I was "too much" to handle. I had to admit I was hurt and needed to speak up for myself at some point to let him know the teasing wasn't received so easily.

As we exercise these new muscles of discernment and self-control, we need to accept the new things God does in our lives and in the world around us. The Lord told us this in Isaiah 43:19 NKJV. *Behold, I will do a new thing, now it shall spring forth; shall you not know it? I will even make a road in the wilderness and rivers in the desert.*

Why do we fight so hard against the new? Why do we get stuck in the old, comfortable and cozy, when we know He is moving and changing things to bring forth heaven on earth continually? Seasons change continually. We need to learn to discern the changing times and seasons and move with God when He moves.

We are in the process of becoming more like Christ. We need to accept and begin the process, even when we don't see the end of it. To maintain a good attitude, one of thanksgiving and joy during the trial, the journey, the process. Too often, we continue lollygagging around the wilderness with the Israelites, whining about how we could be eating the leeks and onions in Egypt, rather than being in awe of the provision of daily manna and the occasional quail.

First, Moses had to lead the Israelites out of Egypt. Then Yahweh had to get Egypt out of His people, which took forty years. How long is it taking you to get through the process you're undergoing?

Where are you on the journey? What level of anointing and faith have you already achieved? It is time we performed up to the level of anointing we've been given. To live a life where we are in that place where we have to TRUST Him. It's called FAITH for a reason. If we want to see the supernatural in our lives, we need to be in a position where miracles are necessary.

My aunt had a meme (back before memes existed) magnet on her refrigerator in the 1980s. It said, "We don't believe in miracles around here. We rely on them." Are you ready to live outrageously for Jesus, you simply *rely* on miracles every day?

We are the temples of the Lord. His glory is within us. Wherever we are should be brightened, illuminated, blessed by our presence. Our hearts should be purified and full of His love, peace and goodness. Seeing supernatural power exercised all around us. Mountains moved, bodies healed and lives changed.

Chapter Thirty-One

Fruit of the Spirit

My children are mean to one other, attacking the ones coming to Me for refreshing, renewal, restoration. They walk in darkness rather than light. They argue, fuss and fight rather than encourage, edify and empower. They do the work of the accuser for him. He has enough minions doing that, he doesn't need more, especially not My beloved ones.

Instead, my desire is for them to walk in love, kindness, peace, joy, goodness, mercy.

Beloved, this starts with you! I want you to set a standard for others, to give the example of life lived for Me. This means you have a closer walk to Me every day, time spent in My presence, focused on Me. As you spend more time with Me, you will shine more brightly with My glory, impacting the world around you for good. You will see atmospheres shift and change with your engagement and involvement there. When you release more love, more kindness, more joy in your home, your community, it will spread like wildfire and others will do the same.

My children are like your box of light bulbs. Different sizes, different wattage, different styles, different shapes, purposes and settings. Different in so many ways, yet alike. Once screwed into place, they will illuminate the area, the room, either a lot or a little. With a particular shade based on their glass cover. Same as My children. Different callings, different purposes, assignments and positions. Each one is similar in standard ways, yet so different in others. You can't mix them up or you'll ruin the fixture, the bulb will blow, you'll throw the breaker, or something adverse will happen. Same for My kingdom. Not being in position according to purpose causes mayhem, wreaks havoc and opens doors to the enemy. Proper fit in the proper place makes all the difference. Yet we can store the bulbs in the same box with no issue, ready for use when needed.

Some people are like hummingbirds, darting around, arms flapping like those wings, swooping around. Others are My eagles, soaring to great heights, riding on My wind currents, resting on My thermals. Using My wind to enable their flights. Others flap constantly, relying on their own strength. Hence, the rise in anxiety and depression. Burnout from NOT relying on Me. Allowing Me to sustain them.

This is the key to going up to new heights. Sustenance, strength. Reliance on Me. Not self. But not many use it currently because they have to relinquish control to gain access. Control has them bound up and restricted. Their actions are limited because of control having so much power over them. As they let go and give up the urge to control everything, they find peace and joy in the simplest things in life, like kitty cats.

This way of life is different. The world is full of people who make excuses, who like to fudge on obedience. Beloved, you must realize to obey a person is to carry out their will, their words.

Don't you know when God reveals something, He expects people to obey Him. Our reaction to the revelation is outward evidence of what is in our hearts.

We need to let this sink in at a level that makes us reevaluate our core. Are we being obedient to what He told us to do? Are we saying what He tells us to say? Are we doing what He instructed?

Prayer is not the end of the journey; it's the beginning. We must be about our Father's business, doing the work He put us on earth to do. Our faith should be producing good fruit.

Let me ask you a question:

Who is in charge of your life? Who do you say yes to every single time?

If you say you follow Jesus, reflect on your deeds, your actions. Do they call you a liar? It is time to let go of childish ways, of who you were before you came to Christ, before you killed your flesh. Now is the time to step into the fullness of who you are in Christ, to fulfill your life purpose.

With God as the reference point in life, how does your perspective shift? Let Him transform you into the fullness of His glory. Stay focused on His mercy and affections for you.

Cultivate each fruit of the Spirit separately in your life.

Love

Evaluate if you're showing love to others through actions. Jesus said,

John 13:35 NKJV *By this all will know that you are My disciples, if you have love for one another."*

Does the world currently know we are disciples of Yeshua? Are we walking in love to the point even the world recognizes whose we are? Or are we so burdened down by busyness, anxiety, depression, bitterness and grudges, we can't begin to love ourselves, let alone anyone else.

- Love better.
- Choose to forgive.
- Let go of the past.
- Put the past in the past.
- Look forward instead.

Joy

Think on joy. Are you feeling weak or lethargic? Seek out His joy. In Nehemiah 8:10 NLT we read,

And Nehemiah continued, "Go and celebrate with a feast of rich foods and sweet drinks, and share gifts of food with people who have nothing prepared.

This is a sacred day before our Lord. Don't be dejected and sad, for the joy of the Lord is your strength!"

Are you pushing through the end of a season, struggling to find the strength to carry on? Stop right now and simply take a deep breath. Inhale the goodness and joy of the Lord. Let it fill you down to your very tippy toes. Wait for it to bubble up out of you.

Father, I ask for fifty-five-gallon drums of joy to be dumped upon the person reading this book right now. I ask for outrageous joy to be poured over each one, drenching them completely in Your strength, letting it seep into every cell, the depths of their being. Thank you, Lord.

You should be the most joyful person in the room. Filled with the Holy Spirit. Then the world will take notice and ask why you aren't stressed out like they are.

Peace

Are you centered in peace? Has the peace that passes all understanding filled your heart, your mind, your soul? How long does it take you to calm down, to reset after an incident? After something happens to try to steal your peace?

Graham Cooke taught on this years ago. We should focus on staying in a position of rest, of peace, so when the world comes at us, we simply step back into position. We develop the ability to be elastic, to stretch out with whatever is the temptation, the challenge, the trial and then pop back into place just like a rubber band.

As you work on this ability, you'll find yourself snapping back into place faster and faster as you grow.

Patience

Don't cringe. Don't growl at me. How are you doing on being patient with yourself, with others, with God? Not just waiting, but waiting with a smile on your face, in your heart. Content in the moment, abiding in His presence.

I've often heard not to pray for patience because it means God will give you opportunities to grow in it instead of just wrapping it up in a nice little box and handing it to you. In response, I'd like to focus our attention on Romans 5:3-5 NLT.

3 We can rejoice, too, when we run into problems and trials, for we know that they help us develop endurance. ***4*** *And endurance develops strength of character, and character strengthens our confident hope of salvation.* ***5*** *And this hope will not lead to disappointment. For we know how dearly God loves us, because he has given us the Holy Spirit to fill our hearts with his love.*

When we encounter challenges and crises in life, we can either collapse in defeat or look to the hills where our help comes from. We can look to Jesus and exercise faith, relying on Him to show up, to provide. In the moment, we exercise patience, graciously waiting in the moment, not haranguing or grumbling about our situation. In doing so, we develop our own character, we strengthen our hope in Christ. It might be why He continues to give us opportunities to grow in patience.

Kindness

Practice one small random act of kindness a day. Even the world tells you to be kind. Are your actions and words laced with kindness? Or bitterness, sarcasm and snark? Sorry to be the one to tell you but sarcasm is *not* a spiritual gift, at least not one from Yahweh. It is time for the Bride of Christ to exude kindness in Her actions and words, to speak life wherever She goes. To speak the truth in love.

Gentleness

Let's review a few scriptures about gentleness.

Colossians 3:12 NLT

Since God chose you to be the holy people he loves, you must clothe yourselves with tenderhearted mercy, kindness, humility, gentleness, and patience.

1 Timothy 6:11 NKJV 11 But you, O man of God, flee these things and pursue righteousness, godliness, faith, love, patience, gentleness.

To be gentle is to have softness of action or effect; lightness. We've dealt with the harshness of the religious spirit within the Body of Christ for far too long. We've endured tirades, lectures, and sermons for centuries. It is time for us to walk in gentleness.

One thing I am continually amazed by is watching friends minister to warriors who have been abused and traumatized intensely by the evil ones. I get to see people who typically are swinging their Sword of the Spirit and charging the gates of hell with no fear totally shift gears into a meek stance of gentleness and tenderness.

When dealing with someone who's been sexually trafficked, someone who survived Satanic Ritual Abuse, you need compassion and mercy at a whole other level. They need to feel the tangible love of Jesus without judgment or condemnation. They need to know they are safe with you. They've been through enough torture and harm; it's time for them to see what compassion and mercy feels like.

Faithfulness

Faithfulness is such a timely word. To be true to your word and do what you said you would do. Did you promise to show up to church to help set things up forty-five minutes prior to start? Then you need to be there forty-five minutes early and ready to work. Did you say you would call on a certain day, a certain time? Did you promise to follow up? Just do it.

To be trustworthy, to be reliable. In the wild wild west days, a man was known to be trusted for his handshake. If you shook on it, it was as good as done. We need to get back to that standard, to be as true as our word.

Can the Father rely on you to do what you said you'd do? To fast and pray when you said you would? Can He?

Self-control

Do you say everything that pops into your head? Do you fast regularly, work out faithfully, take time to be with the Lord? Do you eat healthy or struggle to watch what you eat?

Dictionary via Google gives the definition as: the ability to control oneself, in particular one's emotions and desires or the expression of them in one's behavior, especially in difficult situations.

When you're under stress, what happens? How do you respond? This shows you the true picture of how much transformation and maturing is still needed in your own life.

Cultivating the Fruit of the Spirit in your life takes work and focus, it takes concentration and continual effort. We need people who are bearing the Fruit, displaying godly character in today's world. We've had enough of amazingly gifted people on stage who lacked the fruit, the character of staying true until the end. Each of us is called to come up higher and be more like Christ. Let's do it!

Chapter Thirty-Two

Known by Our Love

The Lord is seeking for ones who are righteous. He is searching for a good man, a good woman. He looks for fully committed servants who have considered the cost to follow Him and have pushed all of their cash to the center of the table, going all in.

We have been fence sitters long enough. We have had one foot in the Kingdom of Heaven and the other foot in the world. Too many of us have tried to keep up with the Joneses, made our careers idols, put family members on pedestals and made them the center of our worlds, instead of Jesus Christ. We have let the fear of man, the lust for approval of man rule our minds, hearts, and ways. Instead of being in the world, we have become of the world.

We have been double-minded in our words and ways. One minute talking of glory and miracles, the next enabling a family member in his addictions, letting one manipulate you into doing things you know are beyond your personal boundaries. We've allowed dysfunction to reside in our homes because we didn't want to hurt feelings, we didn't want to rock the boat. We didn't know how to change. We didn't know life could be different.

It is time to let go of anything that is not of God. It is time to release bitterness and resentment. It is time to remove doubt and fear. It is time to learn to love ourselves, to accept ourselves just as God made us. Jesus told us to love others as we love ourselves. Do you realize the real reason why the world does *not* know us by our *LOVE* is because we don't even know how to love?

OK, let's take a short bunny trail. Since I can already see y'all looking at me like I have three heads. As Graham Cooke would say, "Well, that went down like a rat sandwich." Play the imagine game with me for a moment. I promise we'll be back on point in a New York minute.

If I put a recorder in your mind, if I had a smartphone in your head and could turn on the recording app anytime I wanted, what would I hear? If I could listen to the conversations inside your head, how you talk to yourself, would I need to wash your mouth out with soap? Would I have grounds to arrest you for libel and slander? Would I cringe and cry at the way you talk to yourself? Would you talk to a child the way you talk to yourself?

Would you? Really?

Studies have shown that most people think negatively 60 percent of the time. Guess what, I'll bet Christians are part of that statistic and rarely have a different number. Most of us beat ourselves up regularly. We look in the mirror, and the criticism, the judgment ensues. We discourage, demean and destroy our own hearts and bodies every single day. So, really, much-loved child of the Most High King, please tell me one thing: Would you talk to a prince of the kingdom you are part of in the same voice tone and language you use internally? What if you have to answer to Jesus at the Beta Seat of Judgment about how you spoke ... to yourself?

Looping back onto the main trail again, our baseline, our foundation of life needs to be love. Paul defines what love is and is not in 1 Corinthians 13:4-7 NKJV. There's even a strong chance that you started to recite it from memory when you read the address for that scripture. Say it with me,

4 *Love suffers long and is kind; love does not envy; love does not parade itself, is not puffed up;* ***5*** *does not behave rudely, does not seek its own, is not provoked, thinks no evil;* ***6*** *does not rejoice in iniquity, but rejoices in the truth;* ***7*** *bears all things, believes all things, hopes all things, endures all things.*

Now we know how the Lord defines what love is, let's talk about taking it inside and then outside. We need to walk in the Fruit of the Spirit, which emerges as we allow the Holy Spirit to refine our character. As we are patient with ourselves, kind to ourselves, hopeful and focused on truth, we will see our own mindsets and attitudes change. It starts with asking Papa to show us who He sees when He looks at us. Who are we? Ask Him to remove blinders, demonic filters and lenses you've been wearing. *Listen* to what He says about you.

Quit sniveling. Stop fussing at me. Do not even *think* about rolling your eyes at me. You *need* to grasp this point in order to move forward and get ready for what's next.

OK, I can see you need some proof. I can see that skeptical look you're giving me. Let me share a testimony. My husband, Rob, and I were at a healing conference in Massachusetts a few years ago, and Joan Hunter was ministering to a lady who had chronic illnesses. I think it was fibromyalgia, but it might have been something else. This woman was so ill, she could barely stand up straight; you could just see pain and agony all over her. Next thing we knew, Mama Joan was walking this young lady over to the mirror hanging on the wall. (*OK, what in the world is she doing now?* you might think.)

Joan asked the woman to look in the mirror and say, "You are beautiful and I love you." And then keep saying it. Until she actually sounded like she believed what she said. One seemingly simple step and this woman was healed immediately. Self-loathing, self-rejection, and self-hatred have been running amok in our hearts and minds. It's time to stop that from happening anymore.

Recently I went to the altar during service for an impartation and walked up to Richard Holcomb, the same gentleman who prophesied over Randy Clark thirty years ago the night before Randy trekked to Toronto when and where the Toronto Outpouring began. Richard asked me what gifts I wanted. "Whatever Holy Spirit has for me," was my response.

In the middle of his ministry to me, Richard instructed me to repeat these words, "I love myself." I started to weep. Next thing I knew, he was crying too. I managed to get the words out and had to repeat them several times with confidence before he moved onto the next thing the Holy Spirit had in mind for that day.

I imagine I'm not alone in the struggle to accept myself and love myself just as I am. Are you in the same boat? We have to realize we can't love others when we don't even love ourselves. It is time to kick out self-rejection, self-hatred, self-loathing and learn to love ourselves.

Hear your Father's word for this point:

Get ready, My child. I'm diving in. You see, I have discovered the depths of your heart, the deep recesses of your soul where heartache, despair, doubt, fear, anxiety, self-loathing, self-rejection, self-hatred have collected. I see the contaminated waters. I smell the cesspool where you sent your dreams to drown. That hidden area that no one else suspects even exists. That wellspring of Living Water that has been polluted by words and actions of mankind. I stand here, with a hazmat team of angels; we are here to clean, renew, and restore these waters to pure form. There is nothing to fear, no reason to feel guilty or ashamed. Just say, "Come, Lord Jesus," so I can release My Glory within you.

I'm telling you, you do not realize the impact self-rejection, self-loathing, self-hatred have on your heart, mind, body and soul. It opens the door for the enemy to infiltrate and attack.

According to Henry Wright in *A Most Excellent Way: Be in Health*, self esteem issues lead to:

- Depression and anxiety
- Social phobia
- Attention deficit disorder
- Lupus
- Migraines
- Psoriasis

- Addictions
- Candida
- Rebellion
- Weight gain
- Allergies
- Anorexia & bulimia
- Autism
- Autoimmune diseases
- CFS
- Diabetes
- Endometriosis
- MS
- Prostate cancer
- Rheumatoid arthritis
- Crohn's disease
- And more

Pick up your sword, the Living Word of God, and start fighting back. Start closing doors and sealing them with the Blood of Jesus, so the battle on that front stops finally.

Some of you are still on the fence about this whole touchy-feely love yourself thing. I can tell. So, do me a favor. Hop back to the **Appendix** and read through the I AM scriptures about who you are in Christ and see if you have enough evidence then to believe me.

Once we kick self-rejection, self-loathing, self-hatred, self-destruction, and any other self-deprecating critters to the curb, we can truly walk in joy and love. We allow the Lord to come fill us with His love. We can watch the impact *love* has on our own bodies and minds. Then we get to love others, letting His love flow through us. We learn to express His love. We need to see our own value so we can see the value of ours.

I was diagnosed years ago with one of the worst cases of endometriosis the doctor had ever seen. For those of you who don't know, Endometriosis (en-doe-me-tree-O-sis) is an often painful disorder in which tissue similar to the tissue that normally lines the inside of your uterus — the endometrium — grows outside your uterus. Endometriosis most commonly involves your ovaries, fallopian tubes and the tissue lining your pelvis (Mayo Clinic, 2022). It can cause hemorrhaging, cramps and major blood loss with each menstrual cycle.[1]

Most recently, I started asking the Lord what the roots of this disease was and what I had to do to get rid of it. When I discovered the roots were self-love issues, insecurity and fear, I knew I had some work to do. I'm still working on it. Uprooting decades of self-rejection and self-loathing takes time and effort, but it's sorely needed to open myself up to receive love abundantly.

Won't you join me in learning to fully embrace the Father's love?

---

1. Mayo Clinic. "Endometriosis." October 21, 2022. https://www.mayoclinic.org/diseases-conditions/endometriosis/symptoms-causes/syc-20354656.

Chapter Thirty-Three

Is This My Fight?

He's looking for a few good men. He's searching for a pride of lionesses, ready to chase down some prey. Are you in?

He wants ones who are ready for the outpouring of His Glory, ready for Him to manifest His goodness all around them.

Radical Lovers. Pioneers. Forerunners.

When you get fired up by the Holy Spirit, when the fire has been set inside your bones, you become a Jesus Freak, to use the 1970s term. Suddenly, your flesh tells you to calm down. Be normal. Let's not look ridiculous. What will people think? We don't want to lose cool points. (Fear of Man trying to creep back in.)

Who said we wanted to be normal? It's only the setting on a dryer anyways. We are to be extraordinary. We are to set a new standard of normal that looks like joyful attitudes, supernatural signs all around us, people being healed and set free. And more.

As we start to walk in the supernatural, setting a new standard of normal, we'll find ourselves in situations, in conflicts, in moments where we need to step back and find out a few things. Let's start with asking one simple question:

"Lord, is this my fight?"

King David walked in wisdom in that he would ask the Lord prior to running into battle, "Is this Your will, Lord? Is this what You want me to do?" (Look at the story of Ziklag in 1 Samuel 30.)

Today, we tend to do one of two things. Either we walk away from the fight, not wanting to get involved, to get dirty, to take the time to *DEAL* with the mess, the drama, the warfare involved. We are insecure and lacking confidence in our own ability to defend and fight the enemy. To win.

OR

We rush in where angels fear to tread to every fight in front of us. It's like the fights in the taverns of the Western Movies. We see it start and jump into the fray without thinking of consequences. We don't set healthy boundaries and we step into cow patties regularly because we don't know when to walk away and when to pick up our swords. We don't stop to ask the Lord.

So, Janice, that's nice. I identify with both. I do both. How do I change? What should I do instead?

Glad you asked.

In the heat of the moment, ask the Lord if this is your fight. Ask what He wants to show you and what He wants YOU to do. Shut your mouth and talk to HIM first.

Sometimes, your assignment is to dig in your heels. Stand and fight. Decree a thing and it shall come to pass. Shout, "NO, sir, not on my watch." If you see something, say something. No, I don't mean to turn them into the authorities. I mean, start praying, interceding and waging war over your family, your work, your church, your pastor, your friend, etc. Let out that inner warrior. "It stops here, and it stops now. I'm tired of seeing my friends, my family, my church taken out by ______. It's not happening again on my watch." Then pick up your Sword and FIGHT!

Then again, sometimes it's *not* your fight. Allow me to explain. Occasionally, I have seen posts on social media, desperate for intercession, for prayer. I opened Messenger to send the person a prayer, to actually pray for them at that very moment, when Holy Spirit told me, "No, it's not your fight." I didn't know any details. I didn't know the entire background and story about what was going on. He said no. So, I had to submit. I obeyed and walk away without knowing why He said no.

See, when we pray for someone, we're engaging in the spiritual realm on their behalf. We are raising our swords and joining their fight. We jump into the fighting ring, the arena, with the weapons we have at the ready. When Rob and I were in Honduras on a mission trip, our intercessor team will all testify to the fact it was an intense week. I wasn't the only one under attack that week. Each of them had his/her own battle to deal with. We survived that week *and* we sure learned a lot too.

You stand in the gap when you pray for someone. You want to know you're in the will of God and called to that fight. You need to be assured this is your assignment and your orders are clear. He is the One who gives you the victory.

Too often, we've been caught by friendly fire, attacking our own forces, instead of going after the enemy. We've swallowed the bait.

Chapter Thirty-Four

A Church of Navel Gazers

For centuries, the Church has been dividing and separating, splitting and isolating from each other. The Body of Christ has been hacked into pieces, a right hand here, a left foot there, a kidney over there and a lung over here. We've taken the bait of satan, aka offense, packed it into our suitcases, bought a one-way ticket away from home and moved away. I mean our home church, where we should be connected, valued and equipped. From the days when Constantine declared Christianity to be the state religion and started incorporating paganism into it to the days of Martin Luther, John Calvin and the Wesley Brothers, doctrine and dogma have separated the pieces of the Body for far too long.

We have been concerned about the projected timing of the rapture and arguing with anyone who doesn't believe the same as we do. Far more concerned about *that*, than about advancing the Kingdom of God daily in our life, than about our community members who are hungry, thirsty and impoverished. The world around us needs love, encouragement, and empowerment to be more like Christ.

We have been walking robots, parroting our favorite line, "What about me?" 24/7/365, when the Word of God challenges us to lie down our lives and take up our crosses, and follow Jesus. We have been self-centered, self-absorbed, complete navel gazers while the world goes to hell in a handbasket all around us.

I'm not playing, Church. It is time to wake up and smell the coffee. To fully embrace My teachings and live out My Word.

Isn't it time that we shook the dust off and climbed out of the pity pit we've been in for centuries?

Shouldn't we pick up our shields and swords and step into the battle? It is time to declare: *I want everything Jesus paid for at the Cross.* Nail to the Cross every decree that was spoken against you. Surrender your offenses.

I was recently talking with a fellow author about how witches understand unity and being in one accord way better than we do. They fully grasp the fact they need to focus and come together to accomplish their goals, to pray and fast together to rain down curses and conjure up demons. How is it that the Body of Christ still does not even fathom the power behind being in one accord? Jesus told us, when two or more are gathered in His name, He is there. Do you not think part of that gathering means we're unified?

We've been pretending to be the Lone Ranger or Miss Independent for too doggone long. It is time to recognize we need community, we need each other. Eyes can't survive on their own. Stomachs are of little use if they're not connected to an esophagus and a small intestine. We need each other; we need people with unique gifts and functions to accomplish the task at hand. Get over yourself and get to being about the Father's business.

Chapter Thirty-Five

Welcome Home

Two simple words that evoke such atmosphere shifting. A feeling of refuge, shelter, love, safety, security. A place where you can truly be who you really are. No masks needed. No performance necessary. No putting on a show. No attempting to fit in, to please everyone. Just as you are.

Are you feeling broken, tattered, misused, abused, downtrodden, anxious, depressed, stressed, oppressed, empty? Do you think as if you've nothing left to give?

Welcome Home.

Where your wounds will be treated, your broken heart will be bound up. Your ashes will be exchanged for beauty. Your fears turned in for strength. Your mourning shall turn into gladness. Your despair will be transformed into peace.

Picture it with me.

A father stands with his arms stretched out wide. His daughter lays on her stomach with her feet up, between his legs. He worships; she's covered, protected, guarded.

A man kneels at the altar, struggling and in need of an encounter with Jesus. His brother stands behind him, hands lifted in praise and worship.

A simple stance that says, "I have your back and I've got you covered. Let Him have His way."

I have seen both moments with my natural eyes during worship. I've had the delight of seeing it and reflecting on it with Papa, enjoying the moment of seeing family in action.

The Father says:

I need fathers to arise. I need mature sons of God to come forth. My lost and orphaned sons and daughters are coming home. They need fathers who will love them, heal their wounded hearts and disciple them. To establish safe boundaries for them to grow within. They will deal with rebellion, fear, anxiety, depression, being good enough — fathers will kick out all of that.

You see, a mother gives you life but a father gives you your identity. He calls forth your destiny and tells you who you are. Think about it. Our fathers give us our names. A good father shows love and discipline, boundaries and courage to seize adventure. We need mothers to nurture, to nurse the sick and wounded, to make sure we're eating right and sharing with others. Then we need fathers to call us up higher, to charge us with the call of God, to challenge us to more.

There is something about the feeling you get when a man of God calls you into your destiny, when a father encourages you, empowers you, edifies you into becoming who he sees when he looks at you. Hearing those words, "I'm proud of you. I knew you could do it," fills your bucket in a way not much else does.

On the other hand, there is something about when Dad says to stop that is different than when Mom saying it. I've seen children misbehave, ignoring their mother's admonishments, and when their dad steps in to address the situation, you'd think you'd entered a military base because the young recruits are suddenly attentive and obedient.

Years ago, I played little league softball and my parents were coaches sometimes. My dad worked swing shift and couldn't make every game. But when he was there, you saw a difference in all of the team players, not just me. Something about the support and love of a father makes you want to do better, go higher.

It's time to bring the Spirit of adoption to the fatherless generations. It's time to stand in the gap and open our homes to the widows, the orphans, the neglected. It's time to extend a hand of blessing and acceptance to those who have never known the true love of a father. It's time to be representatives of our Father.

Chapter Thirty-Six

Worship

What if life, every moment of every day, 24/7/365 was all about Jesus? There was no separation between worship, service, work, sports and home life? Think about it. The Holy Spirit is in you and all around you. Life is about living each moment to its fullest. What does He have for you in that circumstance, in that very moment?

He wants to be engaged in your life. Every step you take, every move you make, He is there, waiting to talk with you, waiting to move on your behalf.

A few years back I was training for a triathlon along with several friends from my running group. I remember running around an old Army base that had been closed years before and sensing the angels running through fields with me as I did a 5K loop. As I ran, I began asking Him what the angels were doing. I realized how running would relieve stress, clear my mind and help mental health.

One day, while running by the lake on the base, I heard the Lord say, "Running is a form of worship for you. Denying flesh, saying no to laziness and slothfulness, getting your feet moving and your heart pumping shifts your attitude and is good for you. It enables you to spend time with Me." That puts a whole new perspective on going for a run, doesn't it?!

As you know, there are three legs to a triathlon. Swim + Bike + Run. During training season, I would swim in the local YMCA's pool several times a week. I eventually discovered it was a great time to intercede for others; I could pray while I swam. It gave me something to focus on while swimming laps, rather than simply counting laps. It was a perfect time to just talk with God.

I even had to stop my bike at times in order to take notes of ideas prompted by talking to Papa and riding through Western Maryland.

But He doesn't only use exercise to speak to His children. He can use movies, TV shows, books and more. When you choose not to put God in a box, He can use any way He wants to speak to you. Record your dreams in a journal. Seek interpretation from sound believers or from the Lord Himself. Ask Him to speak to you. And then listen!

Chapter Thirty-Seven

Come Away with Me

There are also times where He wants you to spend time focused and alone with Him. Hear His invitation to come away.

Come Away With Me

Come Away with Me.

Let all the worries and concerns of this earth fall away as you take My hand. Come away with Me. Forget the stresses and fears of this present time. Come away with Me.

Release bitterness. Step out of envy. Break free from the snare of offense. Shatter the glass wall of self-preservation from around you. Come away with Me.

Strife. Division. Distraction. Anger. Fear. Despair. Irritation. Pride. These are all things that do NOT belong to you. Surrender anything that is not of Me at the foot of My Cross. Receive an in-filling of My Spirit to heal your soul, to touch your heart and renew a right spirit within you. I have come to give you a brand-new life, abundant with goodness and mercy.

Come away with Me.

I have prepared a place for us to meet, to be together. It is a place where we can walk and talk together, peaceful, serene, tranquil and full of My Glory. I have much to share with you. Come away with Me.

Do you hear Him calling you, inviting you to sneak away with Him? He wants to spend time with you, where you sit still with Him and simply rest, abide in His Presence. Let His goodness soak into every pore. Feel His love surround you and let His shalom peace flood your soul.

Come, dwell in My Presence. Come sit a spell as Southerners say. Come abide with Me, abide in Me. Allow My Presence to envelop you so you are surrounded by love, joy, peace, security, safety, goodness, mercy, purity, holiness, righteousness, faithfulness, grace, self-control, courage, boldness. Let My Presence surround you. Allow Me to shift your atmosphere to Kingdom-based!

Soak in My goodness. Just as you step into a steaming hot springs pool to be rejuvenated, restored, renewed, step in a pool of glory. Step in. Let the steam arise. Let it clear out your sinuses, cleansing them of worldly toxins. Let the medicinal springs soak away any cares or concerns you brought to the glory pool. Just breathe. Exhale, My child, as worries, fears, anxiety all are gently washed away in the heat of My glory. Allow My glory to seep into every pore as it brings new life to your skin, so your body soaks it in, penetrating the walls that protect you from the dangers out there.

Let Me in. Trust Me. I have blessings, hidden treasures, secrets of the deep waiting for you, waiting for you to be still and wait on Me. Waiting for you to come and dine with Me, abide with Me, be with Me. I have so much to tell you, to share with you, My friend. Set aside time to be with Me, to soak in My Presence. I bring forth the treasures, the gifts, the presents I have set aside for you as rewards for coming close, pressing in, pursuing Me. The more you come after Me, the more goodness and mercy pursue you.

I breathe over you. My breath is sweet, pleasant to your nose. My breath is a wind stirring up the anointing. My breath quickens your spirit. My breath ignites a fire within you that cannot be extinguished. My breath restores. It renews. It redeems. It resets. As I breathe on you, the chains fall off, the ropes that bind you turn into dust, cuffs that hold you captive open immediately. The prison cell that once held you crumbles into the ground as I breathe on you. My breath releases freedom into the atmosphere.

Sit here a minute. Take a deep breath. Feel the chains falling off, the ropes turning into dust and feel the liberation. Breathe in freedom and see how it feels.

Just rest.

Just soak in My Presence.

Just be. Be My child, My little lamb for this moment in time. Let Me hold you close, cradled in My arms.

Just breathe, much-loved child. Breathe in My grace, My peace, My joy, My love, My strength.

Just soak. You don't have to do a thing. Be Mine.

Fully engage your mind, your heart, your soul in this minute. Focus your entire being on Me.

Turn your eyes towards Me. Look freely into My Face. Take this moment to look into My eyes and see My love for you.

Rest in My embrace.

You are strengthened, encouraged and emboldened for My work when you rest in Me, spending time in My embrace.

Beloved, do you realize anxiety is when you reflect on your future and do not see God there? So many of us are anxious, oppressed, depressed and stressed because we are worrying about our future, our family, our finances, our country and not looking to God first. We are not seeking Him first in all things.

OK, that's nice, Janice. I'll admit right along with you that I'm a worry wart. I'm nervous nelly. I struggle with anxiety and have the hives to prove it. So what? What do you want me to do?

Well, I'm glad you asked. Let's talk about worship. He desires our worship. He demands our worship. He is jealous of our worship. He doesn't want us focused on the things, the people we tend to turn into idols. He wants us to solely focus on Him and magnifying Him. Why? Because worship shifts our mindsets and thought patterns. True worship requires us opening our hearts to the Lord, letting go of the self-protection we have because we've been hurt by love before. We must renounce the fear of man, the tendency to worry about what others think about our singing, our dancing, our weeping, wailing, our worship. Silencing the accuser who's been telling you that you're not worthy, not qualified, not good enough, not adequate.

Think about this story in scripture, beloved. The prostitute washed the feet of Jesus with her tears and dried them with her hair. Amid their mockery and appall, she simply worshiped Him.

It's time to approach the altar, the stage, the Mercy Seat of God with your brokenness. Amid their accusations. He will meet you there. Do *not* be content with the shadow side of the veil.

Come into the Holy of Holies; knowing He will meet you there.

He is ravished by your love. His love covers a multitude of sin. Won't you finally recognize that you are a son of God and serve willingly and fully?

Are you willing to be changed? To be changed into a much-loved son?

You are being called to go into deep waters, where feet may fail, where your trust is without borders. Do you know what that looks like? It is uncharted territory. It is walking off the map. It is pioneering new land. It is going into places, doing things you don't fully understand, you don't comprehend.

He is taking you out of the safety zone, where buoys and ropes mark off areas. Taking you deeper, where your only choice is to fully rely on Him. Where you rest in His embrace, where your eyes look to Him instead of at the waves. You look at Him, not the churning water at your feet. Child, you need to learn to focus on higher things. Ignore the waves. Forget about the ground warfare, the drama, the currents of water. Look at Him. Fix your eyes on Him. Find out what He is doing in your situation. Quit paying attention to the enemy, his tactics, his taunts, his temptations.

Place your soul in His embrace. The base of your emotions, feelings, your actions, your perspective, place it in Him. Give it to Him. Let Him cleanse you, purify you, prune you, purge you. A soul resting in His embrace is not depressed, anxious, fearful, doubtful, angry, offended or prideful.

You are full of His Spirit. Bear His fruit.

His glory is falling on holy altars. He is bringing a fresh encounter to the earth. It is time to live in Him and not grow weary. To burn with holy fire inside of us to do His work.

Chapter Thirty-Eight

From Worshippers to Warriors

It is time for My worshippers to become warriors. It is time for those who have soaked in My glory, basked in My presence, sat at My feet, to rise up with wings as eagles, run and not be weary, walk and not faint. It is time for My children to wage war, to fight, to storm the gates of hell and advance My territory, to slay giants. It is time to seize the power and authority I have given to them, to rule and reign on this earth, in this realm.

It is time to step into the new era. The new thing I am doing on this earth. I desire a generation of humble yet confident, strategic yet meek, passionate yet peaceful ambassadors. My children have been enduring sickness, disease and pain, living in suffering for far too long. It is time to find the abundant life My Son died to give them. They shall no longer allow the enemy to steal their health, their joy, their peace.

I saw a command of warriors and their horses standing at the castle, waiting for the bridge to come down so they could ride out. As the worship intensified, the praises went higher. Both troops and their noble steeds became frenzied, ecstatic and ready to run to the scene. Yet the bridge didn't come down.

As the people came into unity, to sing in one accord, in unison, something shifted and the drawbridge lowered. The warriors rode into battle.

This is a vision of the angelic who are waiting on the Bride of Christ to become unified, to become solely focused on the Bridegroom. To learn to worship with our whole heart, with our bodies. To approach the Mercy Seat of God, the Throne Room, as confident sons and daughters of the Living God, ready to show our adoration, our awe, our amazement at who He is.

Do not be content with the shadowy side of the veil. Let's get lost in His Presence. Soak in His love. When you surrender control of your life, your situations, your crisis, you let go and let God, then you have made room for Him to show up. You can step into rest and relax in Him.

Position yourself for connection, blessing, impact. If you want a gift, what do you do? If you are ready to receive something, what does your stance look like? You extend an open hand, waiting. Extend your hand to the Lord. He's waiting for you.

Onto "entering His courts with praise." Did you know our praise is a weapon? Our shout shakes mountains. Our dance changes things. Abstaining from expressive worship hinders our relationship with God. Stop judging others' expressions of worship and focus on your own response to His Glory. Do not let your emotions determine how you worship. Let your worship impact your emotions and your thoughts.

He is worthy.

Paul tells us to rejoice in the Lord always. We are to minister unto the Lord and offer sacrifices of praise. It only makes sense that it's a sacrifice if it costs you something to give it. To praise Him in the midst of the storm, to thank Him for being a good Father even though it doesn't appear to be that way right now. To raise a hallelujah in the presence of your enemies. Despite what you see, you can still trust your God and know He knows what He is doing. He works all things out for good for those who love

Him. The caveat there is that you love Him. If you can confirm to me you love the Lord, then you can trust He is working it out for your good.

Sometimes He is using the trial, the circumstance we are in, to teach us things. He allows the process, the journey to show us things, to take us deeper into Him.

You are learning in this trial, this fire to learn to wage war victoriously. Do not ask Me to rescue you from the mess you are in. Do not ask Me to change your circumstances based on how you think things need to be. Just stop. Just freeze. Do not move. Do not talk. Do not.

Now, beloved, focus on ME! Take your eyes off the situation. Stop focusing on what you see naturally. Stop magnifying what is going on around you. This is not about what others are doing or saying. This moment is about you. Do you hear Me, child? It is about you. Take a deep breath. I am interested in transforming you into the likeness of Christ. That means anything not of Me shall be removed. Amid the challenge, ask Me what I am doing and what I wish to do in you. *Take your eyes off of the chaos, strife, rebellion, division, drama that surrounds you and focus on Me instead.*

I prepare a table of plenty in the presence of your enemies. Let's think about this. If you are going to dine in their midst, you cannot be battling, debating, arguing with them. You have to be in tune with what I am doing instead.

Rise above the ashes. Step out of the boat. Walk on water with Me. Bear My fruit.

Now, remember Isaiah didn't say no weapons would form against you, he just said they wouldn't prosper. Jesus told us we would suffer, we would be tempted, we would go through challenges and crises. He did not promise a rose garden.

I'm sorry. I know you might have thought once you accepted Jesus as Lord and Savior, it'd be a cushy ride. Not so much. We are at war and we have to engage in the battle. We are required to pick up our shield and sword and start using them. Get off the couch. Get out of the chair, the pew, and get to work.

If you want a breakthrough, if you want change, ask the Lord, "What do I need to do? What do I need to change? Who do I need to forgive?" The mountain begins to move when we take a step. Sometimes we're waiting on God to move and He's waiting for us to simply do the thing He told us to do, umpteen times already.

Years ago, I was in a job and I knew it was time for change. I was ready to start something new. I felt the grace lifting for the current position and was ready to go. Yet there I was, stuck in the hallway. A friend finally asked me, "What do you need to release? What do you need to let go of and leave in this season? What are you *not* taking into the next season with you?"

I got quiet before the Lord and asked Him these questions. *What behavior had I been doing, what actions, what expectations, what attitudes needed to be taken out of my toolkit, my tackle box and left behind in the past?* After I worked through these questions with the Lord, I suddenly got a phone call asking me to come in for a job interview. Within a month or two, I was starting a new job that was much closer to home and matched the dream job description I had drafted earlier that year with Papa's help.

Amid our situations, we need to fix our eyes on Jesus. Crank up the warring worship music and get to dancing. Start shouting. You see, beloved, your worship changes your thinking, changes your attitude. When you take your eyes off yourself, off your problems and put them on Jesus, you begin to shift atmospheres, starting with your own.

How do you worship, how do you continue to praise Him when you don't feel like it? Grab the milk and cookies. It's storytime again.

Years ago, Rob and I went through three in vitro fertilization attempts. I remember getting the phone call the final result was negative, we weren't pregnant. All the waiting, the hormone injections, the egg retrieval and processing hadn't worked. I felt like a failure yet again.

At that moment, I curled up on the couch and just cried. I didn't understand what went wrong. I couldn't fathom why it worked for others, but not us. I hoped and my hope was deferred, making my heart sick. Yet, I ran to Him. Unable to comprehend but choosing to rest in Him and fall into His arms. To choose to praise Him in the midst of pain, I found a new level of worship known as lamentations, a tender and sweet praise that touches the heart of God. Where His beloved chooses to adore Him in the midst of agonizing pain.

It is not easy to choose to run to Him in those moments. Flesh demands answers and wants to be heard. The enemy whispers so many reasons why you should hate God, why you should walk away, why you can't trust Him anymore, why why why. Even trusted friends say the wrong things.

In that moment, I discovered the truth of how the only safe and secure place to be was in the arms of Jesus. To run to Him and say, "Though You slay me, yet I will trust in You."

Chapter Thirty-Nine

Thy Word I have Hid in My Heart

What if the verse *Thy word I have hid in my heart that I might not sin against thee* isn't just about memorizing Scripture? What if it is about the words He gives us? The personal prophecies, the identity words, the destiny words dispatched to us over the years. The ones we've cultivated, processed, distilled so much, they're hidden as treasures in our hearts. If we know what He has called us to, how could we choose anything but Him, following Him, doing His will, fulfilling His assignments?

Totally changes the intent and feeling in that passage, doesn't it?

What have you done with the prophetic words you've received over the years? Have you rejected them because they sounded too good to be true? Have you chewed on them and taken them to the Lord for judging? Have you dove into them for treasures?

There is a smorgasbord awaiting you in the depths of prophetic words. You just have to do the chewing.

Chapter Forty

Watch Your Mouth

"Watch your mouth!"

We probably heard it a thousand times, yet I don't think we ever realized the reality, the Biblical principle behind that command our parents gave us throughout our childhood.

> "Death and life *are* in the power of the tongue, And those who love it will eat its fruit." Proverbs 18:21 NKJV.

Do we live as if we believe that verse to be true? Do we realize the curses we speak over ourselves and our families and others? When we say, "My back is killing me." "That kid will be the death of me." "If that happens one more time...." We are declaring death, disease, destruction over ourselves and our lives with every word we speak in this vein.

What if we truly embraced the reality we have Resurrection Power inside of us, we can create or destroy with the words we speak? God spoke the universe into existence. What do we speak into existence or out of existence with our words daily? What impact are our words having on the world around us?

Sticks and stones may break my bones, but words will never hurt me. We chanted this mantra as children when someone snarked something mean to us. It is time to realize the mantra was a lie from the pit of hell. Ask a husband, berated and demeaned by his wife daily. Ask a teenager whose parents constantly criticize and ask why he can't be more like his sister. Ask a pastor's wife who is judged and scolded by the church folk every week. Ask anyone who's been emotionally, mentally abused.

It's time to realize tormentors play mind games with their words in order to break the spirit of the captive. It's not just physical torture; it's about the trauma to their minds and souls they can cause. Often, a person can withstand the physical pain but the mind games, the verbal assault is what breaks them down. The enemy knows this and uses it to his advantage because much of the Body of Christ has been ignorant or in denial to this principle.

> So shall My word be that goes forth from My mouth; It shall not return to Me void, But it shall accomplish what I please, And it shall prosper *in the thing* for which I sent it. Isaiah 55:11 NKJV (italics added)

If His words go forth to accomplish something, to prosper, don't you think our words also do the same? We speak things into existence. We call them forth. Controlling our tongues, watching what we say becomes easier the more we worship Jesus, the more we praise God.

When Joshua led the Israelites around Jericho, they marched in silence for six days. Now why do you think they were ordered to be quiet? Well, let's think about why Zechariah, father of John the Baptist, was mute for the months leading up to John's birth. He doubted the word of God delivered by His angel.

I can just hear the angel's response. "OK, Zecky, you've done it this time. You picked the wrong time to be doubtful of God's promises. Let's see what you believe and speak by the time your son is born."

My suspicion is this: The Israelites are known in Scripture to be a fussy, whiney bunch. So the Lord had to give them a gag order so they wouldn't undermine their own authority in His warfare strategy for taking down Jericho.

"Obviously their mouths get them into trouble, so we're gonna have to ensure they don't talk themselves into a mess again. I'll have Joshua issue the vow of silence command."

> "Always keep your words soft and sweet, just in case you have to eat them." ~ Andy Rooney

Words manifest into real life. Think about it. Let's go back to Genesis 1. In the beginning, God created. Grab that Bible or open your app of choice on your mobile device and look it up. Now, tell me, how did God create? Did He dump a bunch of chemicals into some test tubes? Did He throw a bunch of ingredients into the Kitchen-aid mixer? Did He gather all the right construction supplies in accordance with the blueprints?

No?

Then, what *did* He do?

God spoke and it came into existence. Sun, moon, stars, planets, seas, land, mountains, valleys, fish, birds, animals ... all of it came into being with a few words. Let there be ____ and there was.

OK, since we've established we agree on God's words having the power to create, let's move onto the next piece of the puzzle. You have the power of life and death in your tongue. (Go read the book of James if you need some scripture to back it up). You have the Resurrection Power inside of you. (Don't mind me. I'm just over here, asking Jesus to stoke the fire in your soul a wee bit, use one of those fans that blow oxygen into the fire so it burns hotter, burns higher. Alright, alright, enough fooling around. Let's focus.)

Would you allow me to follow you around for a day, even just an hour, so I could record what you say to yourself, your family members, your coworkers, your pastor, and dare I even mention what you comment on social media posts? Are your words blessing or cursing, encouraging or discouraging those in your sphere of influence? Sweet pea, might I ask *WHAT* are you calling into existence in your life?

Are you expressing gratitude, kindness, gentleness, authenticity, transparency, honesty? Let's bring your hopes and dreams into the conversation.

No, sit back down. No running away from me now, sweets. Take off those running shoes. The Bible tells us hope deferred makes the heart sick. Maybe you're like Joseph and you had these dreams, these visions, of being appreciated, recognized for greatness, adored as a youth. Maybe you're Hannah and you've been hanging out in the temple, crying out for a child with a priest whose only thought is you're drunk. Maybe you're David, a slayer of lions and bears, yet your own father doesn't even think of you when the prophet comes to anoint the next king, your older brother thinks you're prideful and arrogant when you're simply full of righteous anger at the indignant giant running his gums.

Wait, hold up, did you believe the lie of the worm that said you were the ONLY one to get thwarted, to end up in prison, to see your dream die on the vine instead of becoming wine? Did you take the bait that said you were unique in your gloom and doom? Aren't you cute?

Before you think I'm rude, snarky and the cruelest person you know, permit me a page or two to defend myself. You see, I have been there. I have the t-shirt, actually about three or four of them by now. I have battled anxiety, depression, infertility, hostile work environments, sexual harassment in the workplace, childhood sexual abuse, betrayal by friends and loved ones, ignored and unseen so. Many. Different. Times.

I could list so many trials and valleys I've journeyed through. Tell you about the days, the nights I spent facedown on the carpet in that little mountain church, crying my eyes out while crying out to God. Then picking myself up, wiping my face and walking into dinner with the church folk.

I could tell you about the heavy oppression cloud I was under, one so horrible I actually heard an audible voice ask me, "Why are you crying out to HIM? He doesn't love you anyways." How I crumbled on the stairs in defeat, stunned at such a thought. Granted, the phone rang within minutes and it was a friend who helped get my head on straight (or as a Texan would say, "Get my mind right). Our loving Father told me afterwards, "Why did you believe that worm? You *know* better." Reminding me of our relationship and the legacy of a life spent with Him.

Then there's the rocky times of marriage where I grumbled more about my husband than I graced him with my words. When I was focused on what annoyed me and how he irritated the snot out of me. How suddenly I was surrounded with friends who spoke life and flipped the script to the things they saw in him, what they liked about it, how amazing he was. My friends helped me to recall the good, and let go of the bad.

So, I know the isolation tactics, the you're-the-only-one belief system the worm likes to use on the Bride of Christ. Plus, I know it's one big lie from the pit of hell. Don't you think it's time we stopped falling for it?

It is time to wake up and smell the coffee. It is time to get our helmet of salvation on correctly and let it do its job protecting and guarding our minds.

Chapter Forty-One

Who Has Your Attention During Worship?

Ever been in a worship service where you found yourself criticizing the fashion attire of the worship team? Ever discovered yourself evaluating and critiquing the scriptural accuracy of the sermon? Been annoyed with the light and smoke show happening in front of you?

If not, bless you. You don't battle the judgmental, critical spirits the way I have. If you have, this chapter is for you. Here's a word Papa gave me one time I was in that very mood.

Are you here to assess the performance, be entertained, judge the worship team, the preacher's sermon OR are you here to worship Me?

What is your intent? Which is your focus?

You make the choice. Either be intentional about your praise and worship or you will be distracted by the enemy easily. You can always find an imperfection with an imperfect vessel. What has your attention?

Well then, how about that? Isn't it time that we listened to what others are saying? Shift our focus and determine how we can help, how we can meet their needs. We are all selfish unless we do something about it.

We all need to be careful on how you talk to others. It's time to treat others, including those in your own household, with honor and respect.

Chapter Forty-Two

Epic

An epic story has an epic conflict. You're going through this conflict because He has an amazing story He wants to tell through your life. He is using this conflict to remove certain roots from your heart. As you bare your heart and soul to Him in the midst of your trials, He is able to cut out the dead flesh, remove the heart of stone and replace it with one that beats when His beats. He can cleanse you of transgressions and iniquity that have plagued you and your family for decades if you allow Him to operate. He wants to transform you into the likeness of Christ. He then uses your life trials for His glory. He redeems all things.

Metalsmiths place the metal from the mines into the fire to burn off impurities. As the yucky stuff bubbles to the surface, the smith scrapes it off and puts it back into the fire. This process continues until the metal is refined and purified. It is time to be delivered from bitter root judgments and to awaken the warrior within. To let the fire blaze within our very souls, so it bubbles up that bitterness to the surface and the silversmith can remove it. To emerge from the fire as a loving and kindhearted person who shines, reflecting the glory of God.

As we let go of bitterness and resentment, we can embrace love and joy, peace and kindness. Do you hear Him calling?

He's calling us deeper, deeper into the wells of joy.

He is calling us out to the depths of oceans of love.

He's calling us onto the white waters of the rivers of mercy and grace.

He's calling us to the stillness of His lakes of glory.

Don't you see Him standing there, staring at His beloved with eyes of Love and fire, waiting for Her to respond, for Her to come, to come with Him?

Will you leave the shores of safety?

Will you release the ties that bind you to the banks of the rivers?

Will you let go of what's known to follow Him into the unknown?

Will you put your hand in His and just go, content to be wherever He is.

Will you walk in the days numbered for you?

He wants to irritate us with His dreams about us.

Provoke an itch that doesn't let us rest until we venture out beyond our comfort. Out with Him, where you can't see the bottom, where you have no hope of touching bottom anymore. Where ships sail and sea creatures lurk. Out with Him.

Waves come. Winds blow. Storms rage. Sharks may circle. Pirates may attack. Supplies for the journey might look sparse. Injuries may come because of the danger zone you have entered. The possibilities are endless.

One thing is sure: He is with you. He will never leave you nor forsake you. If you stay focused on Him, and not the winds, the waves, the raging storm, the circling sharks, or the prowling pirates. You shall remain content and peaceful, abiding in Him. As you rely on Him to provide for every need every step of the way, you get to see supernatural provision. Miracles happen as He moves mountains on your behalf. The adventure, the excitement, the joy, the delight of this journey can only be experienced if you go, if you say "yes!"

Chapter Forty-Three

Sonic Boom

I hear a sonic boom breaking the sound barrier. A time of acceleration has arrived. You are about to take off at such a speed, your flight breaks the sound barrier. The brass ceiling, the barrier the enemy had built to block the Voice of the Lord from His children, your takeoff shatters it completely. As the pieces fall to the ground, the warriors pick them up, transforming the pieces of barrier into individual ear plugs, filters to block out the voices of the enemy. Repurposed for good.

He is releasing his battering rams upon the earth. If you are one of His battering rams, you need to understand that battering rams are used to break through the gates of the enemy's fortresses. Your assignment is to open a pathway for the soldiers to enter, not to go inside the fortress. Rams break through the gates. There are warriors coming forth who will break through the gate so others can go inside.

Understanding one's assignment and purpose is critical to completing it successfully. Breakers are called to be trailblazers, making a pathway for others to follow. They are not called to settle, to build a house and remain there. They are to pioneer new territories and enter new lands.

If you are a pioneer, a battering ram, please do not be surprised when others follow you, retracing the trails you have blazed, stepping inside buildings that you battered down the way in. You were sent to break into, to blaze through so that others could follow and execute their assignments.

It's time we worked as a unit, a team, instead of lone rangers. Different assignments don't mean one is any more important or worthy than the other. Recognize different assignments, gifts and abilities. Make room for others to jump in and engage as the Lord leads, flowing in grace.

Chapter Forty-Four

I Determine Your Worth

I determine your worth.

I decide the value placed upon you.

Your worth, your value is not based on man's opinions, man's judgments, man's criticisms of you.

It is not even based on your own opinions and judgments against yourself.

Surely your enemy has no authority over determining your true value, your true worth.

I am the only one who gets to determine this, for I am the One who paid the ultimate price for your life, a life now spent in eternity with Me.

I have determined you are more precious than diamonds, more treasured than rubies. You are Mine. The world tries to place a value upon a life. Medical doctors, human traffickers, insurance companies are among those who attempt to determine life's value, its worth. But they are not qualified to do so, for they are not the creator of life, the giver of life.

Only I have the authority to establish your worth and I have done so with the price of sacrificing My Son so you could spend eternity with Us.

Do not let anyone else define you. Be faithful to do what I have called you to do.

Shall we return to the discussion of **Chapter 32** where I talked about self-esteem, self-rejection and its impact upon our bodies? It drills down to the fact we undervalue ourselves, not recognizing the price paid for our redemption and reconciliation with the Father. We cannot see ourselves as royalty, as pearls of great price. If we simply caught a wee grasp of the true value He sees in us, we'd never accept the enemy's taunts and tirades as truth again.

Chapter Forty-Five

Start a War

He's coming in to start a war.

When you invite Jesus into your heart, your mind, your body and soul, He comes in and starts a war. He floods the place with His blood. He has a battle plan to take every hill, every stronghold, every high place inside of you. He is claiming every territory as *HIS*. Every test, every trial, every victory, every defeat you experience is His battle. He is engaging in battle with your spirit to take on soul and flesh. He is defeating every flesh part left inside of you, every bit of your soul, until you're fully redeemed. ALL of you. He's focused on tearing down every stronghold, platform, fortress within that prevents Him from being Lord and Savior fully and completely. When you battle negative thoughts, when you go to war over old habits that need to break, when you feel the inner struggle raging inside of you, realize it's Christ, your lover, and surrender. Let Him reign freely.

Beloved child of God, you have been waging war over the fulfillment of your destiny since before you were born. The enemy has been trying to steal, kill and destroy it and you all along. Your dreams are not too big, dear heart. Stop and ask the Lord right now what He thinks of you, what He wants you to do. He designed you for a purpose and a plan. It's time to walk out what you were called to do.

You don't want to get to heaven and hear, "I had more for you, but you didn't think you were good enough, you were qualified. It was too good to be true, you thought. You self-selected out of My plans for you."

Grab your sword and lop off the head of the spirit of death attacking your destiny. Fight fire with fire. Embrace your identity and purpose on this earth and go after it with everything you've got. Advance His Kingdom everywhere you go.

People are waiting for your spark to ignite them. Their freedom, their liberty is tied to your calling, your walking into your destiny.

Chapter Forty-Six

Fear of the Lord

Are we to fear the Lord when we have been afraid of anything and everything else under the sun? Is that why fear is rampant in the world today? Fear of man, fear of failure, fear of death, fear of loss?

> "Fear of failure is a key tactic of our enemy to keep us on the sidelines and inhibit the inheritance of our destiny. Kings, prophets, and disciples all succumbed to it at times ... and provided priceless stories of the goodness of God's response.

> "Nothing has changed. A people without fear, who will risk because they are so greatly loved, are highly dangerous and will face resistance. We understand that while we may stumble, we cannot ultimately fail because we are aligned with the One who has already won the war. We have permission to try, to learn and to grow stronger in the process. The power of old histories of loss are being swallowed by New Man encounters with outrageous grace and perfect love."

> "We are not alone in this process and it is worth entering and remaining in the arena to behold. We are encountering, comprehending and establishing the quiet confidence of the Mind of Christ; individually and together. We are becoming a people for whom all things are possible because of who Jesus really is; an army in training to take God's fight to the enemy – and win." ~ Allison Bown

Fix your eyes on Jesus. We sang the old hymn about fixing our eyes on Jesus, letting the things of the world grow strangely dim as we looked into His wonder face for decades. Did we ever truly consider the words we were singing? Did we realize the song was telling us a key for overcoming and taking risks successfully? See, when we are captivated by our Lord, our circumstance, the obstacles before us suddenly disappear. We navigate through the situation graciously, in such a way, those around us watch and wonder how we did that.

Rejoicing and thanksgiving are the standard operating procedures of being focused on Jesus. I mean, really, can you see yourself standing there grumbling and mumbling when you are standing before the King? If you think so, might I ask if you really know who He is? Omnipotent, omnipresent, Creator of the Universe, Most High King. The one who has the power and authority to execute justice and judgment.

His holiness, His majesty was so remarkable, unless you were one of the Levitical priests called to carry the ark of covenant on poles on your shoulders, (1 Samuel 6:1-9) you weren't permitted to touch the ark. In today's world, we've lost comprehension of such respect, such honor for holy things. The Israelites were carrying royalty and deity when they carried the ark of covenant. Just as kings and queens would have been carried on litters, Yahweh wanted His presence to be carried with honor and respect. The 10 Commandments, a piece of manna and Aaron's rod were stored inside the ark. Yahweh expected His people to treat His ark with respect and decorum, not flippancy and disregard.

Rewind and understand why the Israelites were taking the ark *back* home. They had lost the ark to the Philistines in battle. One has to wonder if they properly had respect and honor for the ark prior to battle, fully comprehending the significance, the magnitude of what was in the ark and whose presence, they would have acted differently.

Fully understanding the complexity and awesomeness of our Lord inspires fear within man's hearts. A friend on Facebook recently posted about the Fear of God as I was revising this section, so I asked if he could share more on the subject. Here's Chris Bennett's take on the Fear of God:

> I'm always being asked what I mean by, or what is, the Fear of God, or the Fear of the Lord? This is just my take on it. It's probably not theologically correct, but it's my take. The Bible warns us: "It is a fearful thing to fall into the hands of the living God." Hebrews 10:31 NKJV. So how can we fall foul of God in such a way, we disappoint or even anger Him?
>
> My greatest fear of God is that I misrepresent Him prophetically with the words and visions that I publish. I fear God in that way. Another way I fear Him is to fail to do what He calls me to do. This can be when I speak wrongly, or act wrongly, or fail to do as He asks, whether by doing something different by design or accident. I fear God in the way I act as I don't want to fall into sin, nor do I want to behave flippantly or carelessly before Him. I want to revere God in all that I do, or say, or even think.
>
> It's the reverential fear of God that, I hope, drives me in everything I do.

Let's define fear of God. Mostly, I'm referring to the reverential fear. We, my wife and I, tend to keep very short accounts with the Lord. We take communion daily. Reflecting Paul's admonition to examine ourselves, we repent quickly and, usually, daily. I'm not saying for one moment we're squeaky clean, because we're not, but we try to keep fairly clean before Him. We don't mean fear as in scared, but more along the lines of being concerned about not offending God. Although there are moments when real fear does try to invade a situation, but He soon quenches that!

"Fear of God" has a few meanings, but only the lost need fear Him as in scared, as the saints should only fear His displeasure. The only time I will truly fear Him is when I hear the one in front of me told, "Away from Me, I did not know you!" - for that is the scariest thing to hear, ever!

We need to get back to a lifestyle of living in awe of the Lord, walking in respect of His holiness and righteousness. It's time to embrace the reverential fear of God, choosing to act, behave and live accordingly.

When you have an understanding of the Fear of the Lord, you're then ready to lay your life down for Him.

Chapter Forty-Seven

I Need Ananiases

I need Ananiases, consecrated friends of God who are willing to lay hands on My Sauls, to anoint them and call them to their work in My Kingdom, to commission them for their purposes, to prophesy to them their futures, not fearing man's response. I need servants willing to reach into danger zones and call forth My chosen ones. I need encouragers, empowerers, to step up to the plate and knock it out of the park. My warrior champions are ready to be selected. Who will go to where they are and choose them for Me?

Where are the ones ready to be Freedom Brothers?

The world wants real, authenticity, transparency. They're done with hypocrisy and masks. Had enough of happy faces that hide the hidden brokenness inside. It is time to be boldly faithful and true, to be of good courage. I am launching you into your destiny.

Elisha burned the plows when he left the farm to follow Elijah. In 1319, Cortez invaded Mexico, burned the ships and conquered the land. There was no plan B. (Check out the song *Burn the Ships* by For King and Country.)

It's time to cut the ties to the past, to the things that hinder us, that delay us, that dissuade us from our calling, our destiny in the Kingdom. We have allowed pain, trauma, history to program us into robots who repeat the narrative, who simply do what we're told to do, obey our demonic masters that do not want us to see who we really are, the power we truly have. We dwell in the cave, the pit, the prison rather than walking out into freedom. The King was crucified, buried and resurrected so we could be restored to original design. We have been given the keys to the Kingdom, given the power and authority to take dominion.

Yet we stay in our shacks of despair, greed, lust, anger, bitterness and anxiety, wondering why we're stuck in ruts and even 4WD doesn't get us out of them. We keep driving in the same tracks, wondering why we never arrive some place different. We're continually going down the same pathway, clueless as to why things don't change.

It is time to burn the plow and make some Texas Beef Brisket for the neighbors. It's time to turn those ships into kindling for a nice bonfire. Stop allowing your heart wounds, past failures, mistakes and wrong choices hinder your new life in Christ. Quit using the excuse of family baggage and dysfunctional home life to impede your forward movement on the battlefield. Either His love covers a multitude of sins or God lied. Either His Resurrection means you are free or Jesus suffered for nothing.

Stop letting the enemy use your heart, mind and soul as a playground. Tear down the carousel, the monkey bars, the jungle gym and build a fortress of goodness, grace, holiness and mercy instead.

People are waiting for *you* to live in the fullness of your God-given identity. What if your prayers are the ones needed to open doors to a new job, a new home? What if your smile convinces someone to give life another chance? What if your hug squeezes pain, sickness, and disease away for good? What if your words spark a fire within someone called to do great and amazing things? What if you actually could make a difference?

There's a price to pay to serve the Lord, to be fully committed. You must lay your life down, give up the right to choose, to have an opinion, to demand respect and honor. You choose to be a bond-slave to your Creator, saying, "Not my will but yours, Lord." Every single day. You learn to listen more and ask better questions. To focus on developing relationships, affirming others in who God says they are.

Chapter Forty-Eight

Apostles & Prophets Are Coming

There is an awakening of My apostles and prophets occurring. An Apostolic Reformation is happening across the land. I am restoring the fivefold ministry to the Body of Christ. What the Church has seen with the fivefold offices in the past few decades has been the first fruits of the Harvest. It is the water I am using to prime the pump to release the outpouring, the flow of Apostles, Prophets, Teachers, Evangelists and Pastors who are awakening now. The numbers of this harvest are unfathomable. The wickedness of this coming time was unthinkable just ten years ago. Let alone twenty or thirty. As you know, My child, the universal church has not seen the apostles and prophets in full function, operating in selfless ministry.

Man has been stuck in self-absorption and self-centeredness for far too long. Much of the tests and trials facing My children these days is to eradicate a focus on self from their minds. To stop the navel gazing. I need to prepare their minds for the days ahead. Leaders, teachers, shepherds have been focused on self; the church had no example to follow for selflessness. Very few truly walk in surrender and humility, in holiness and righteousness. The move of rising up prophets and apostles in recent times has been preparing ones to teach, to lead, to model the manifestation, the restoration of the fivefold across the globe, in all churches.

I am changing styles, forms and patterns. I am like the Big Bad Wolf blowing down the little pigs' houses of sticks and straw, even the brick ones. It is time for My Church to awaken, to be restored to Her destiny and purpose on earth. Some may fight this shift, kick against the ox goads just as Paul did. It is to be expected; My children have not learned to embrace change, to focus on Me instead of normal life. Their opinions and attitudes will not impede this move of God on earth. They only impact their involvement in it; their future reward in heaven. Few have seen what My children empowered, impassioned and encouraged look like on this earth, walking with Me daily. The world is not prepared, not ready to deal with them either. HA! The church isn't, let alone the world. Yet I am preparing them for release even now. Now is the time to get serious, to focus like a laser, to dig in deeper, like never before.

I will raise My beloved warriors, My generals and admirals, My chosen ones into positions of honor, power and control. I know they are not seeking these things for themselves, but fully surrender it all on My altar. I call them friends. I trust them with My Word. My Word has the power to create or destroy in a second. Therefore, these have endured many tests and trials. They've been through the refiner's fire multiple times. They are chosen for sanctified service.

I see an army arising.

Cloaked in wisdom and majesty. Armored with righteousness and holiness. An army that has been tested and tried, trained and equipped for battle. Not a hodgepodge, hopeless unit, but a battleworthy, blessed group of warriors ready for the fight prepared and empowered.

No one is jockeying for position. No one is trying to outperform others. Each one knows his rank and file. Each one knows his assignment, her duty in the battle. Victory requires them to move in unity, in one accord, knowing they need each other to complete their mission.

Jesus told us that He is the vine and we are the branches. Do we realize branches are fully dependent on the vine for life? The branches are supported by the trunk. A branch cut off from the tree bears no fruit and quickly dies by itself. Any good produced by the branch is solely due to the life-giving sap of the vine. Yielding to the vine and remaining open to the life flowing forth provides sustenance for growth and blossom, fruit and life.

Diving into this analogy shows us how we are utterly dependent upon the Lord. We need to remain in a place of yieldedness to the Holy Spirit. Our lives glorify Him when the radiance of His light shines through every bit of us.

> Unless we know God's fiery presence in our souls, we can be scholars but never worshipers. He delights to reveal His eternal wisdom to your seeking heart and His ravishing splendor to your soul. He has placed within us a new upward passion, a restless yearning to worship Him. The Spirit eagerly awaits us to rejoin Him in the dance. Repentance is turning a cold shoulder to those whom we've allowed to seduce us away from our original partner, and then rejoining Him in the dance of the ages. ~Dwight Edwards, *Revolution Within*

As Eugene Peterson so eloquently put it, "There is no doubt that the Christian life is a dancing, leaping, daring life."

Chapter Forty-Nine

It Only Takes a Spark

When an opportunity presents itself, it's too late to prepare. ~Mark Chironna

Your calling requires commitment. You have to push past the opposition you're encountering. The time for hiding and being fearful is way over. The time for doubting self and God, the time for not believing the *truth* about who you really are in Christ, the facts that you were known before you were formed in your mother's womb, you were born for such a time as this, is now gone. We have entered a new season, a new era. It is time for the ekklesia, the Body of Christ, to step into the fullness of who they are. To walk in abundance, Resurrection Power, to see supernatural signs and wonders everywhere they go. It is no longer extraordinary to see lives changed in a moment because you stopped to share an encouraging word with a person battling depression. It is not unusual to see healing miracles happen in the grocery stores, the ball field, the classroom. We need to start living in the expectancy of the goodness of God to show up every moment of every day.

All of creation is crying out for the Sons to arise. We are the Sons of God creation is waiting for. Just like we sang in Sunday School decades ago, *I'm gonna let my little light shine*. It's time to shine for all the world to see.

Have you ever attended a candlelight service, one with absolutely *no* electric lights on in the room? There is a little chapel in Emmitsburg, Maryland, that hosts Christmas Eve services every year, on the hour, every hour until midnight. There is no electricity in the building. Sconces are lit and placed on walls around the room, but it's dimly lit for almost the entire service. Then, each person gets a candle and the flame is passed from person to person, until the entire chapel full of people is brightened by the illumination of each single light joining together to shine.

If each of us asked the Holy Spirit to ignite our own fire within, make the effort to kindle the flames of others around us, and started burning brightly wherever we are in the world, we just might change the world. Darkness has to flee when the Light of the World shows up. It's time we started showing up with our little lights shining.

Let's stop berating the darkness. Let's stop stumbling about in the darkness. Let's stop allowing the darkness to creep into our homes, schools, cities and countries. Let's eradicate darkness from within our churches by shining brightly. Let's take our little candles and go light the world as Kathy Troccoli sang.

People are waiting for your spark to ignite them. Their freedom, their liberty is tied to your calling, your walking into your destiny. Strike a match and let it burn.

Chapter Fifty

Mind Control

The enemy has tried to control our minds for years. Paul taught us 2000 years ago to take every thought captive to the mind of Christ. We have a helmet of salvation as part of our spiritual armor for a reason.

A key strategy of the enemy is to plant demonic thoughts, seeds of doubt, fear, self-inadequacy, self-deprecation, self-loathing, fear, and so on in our minds. Tormentors whisper in our ears that things will never change, the promises of God are actually just jokes. They tell us hurt, abuse, confusion, chaos, trauma is the way of life on this earth. They tell us we are empty inside, lonely and unloved. They tell us we are fat, ugly, stupid, unwanted and of little to no value. Have I identified one of the key whispers you hear daily yet? Or should I keep going?

These weasels run their lips, tormenting and torturing the children of God with horrible thoughts. Many of us jump onto these trains of thought, without realizing which train in the station we just boarded. Suddenly, we're hundreds of miles away from anything godly, holy, pure or righteous. Mentally, we have wandered so far away from being in alignment with the Lord, abiding in His Presence.

The next thing we don't even know, we are speaking those demonic thoughts out loud. We are releasing curses of death, destruction, demise and discord over ourselves and others, not even realizing the power of our very own words. We have the power of life and death in our tongues. *Think,* beloved, just think about it. The entire world was created with *words.* Yahweh created us in His image. We have the Holy Spirit within us. Whatever we speak, we call into existence. We create with our words. The Word tells us to decree a thing and *it shall come to pass*. Oh, that the Body would grasp the power of the very words we speak.

How often have you heard a wife say her husband is just one of the kids? She adds him to the count of children she has. If she only realized she's cursing him to walk in immaturity and demeaning his role as man of the house with her words. How often have you heard the husband make sarcastic remarks about his wife? She certainly doesn't feel love and adored, protected and secure in that statement. Have you ever heard parents berate umpires or coaches? Have you heard grandparents berate their children in front of their grandchildren? Shall we even discuss the gossip, slandering and judging that the congregation does about its pastor/worship leaders/teachers?

Let's take it to the streets. Then we have what *we (the church)* say about our own supervisors, local police officers, teachers, bosses, governmental officials (Yes, I know, I hear you. The struggle is real. But we are called to speak *life* over our communities and homes, not death.) What if? What if we *stopped* fussing, complaining, whining and grumbling? What if we, instead, choose to sing a new song? What if we began to shift the atmosphere in our own homes, workplaces, churches, communities by putting a filter, a muzzle on our own mouths?

In middle school, I wore braces to straighten my teeth. They came off in ninth grade. Then, for a long while, I had to wear a retainer to hold the teeth in place until they learned their new places. One time, like so many other peers of mine, I had wrapped my retainer in a napkin at a church picnic, and it got thrown away with the paper plate when I was done eating. My mom and I had to go dumpster diving to find that blessed retainer. Those things were expensive.

As an adult, I would often dream I was wearing the retainer. I would dream I lost it and couldn't find it anywhere. I dreamed about that thing *a lot*. Finally, I began to ask the Lord why. What was this recurring dream theme about? The light came on and the obvious answer arrived. He was telling me that He had a spiritual retainer for my mouth and was training my mouth to speak in the Kingdom of Heaven language. Once I figured out the meaning of the dream, I never had it again.

OK, back to our minds. The dark one has so much evil programming in the world. Violence in video games, movies, and TV shows has desensitized a generation to violence. There are now stories of women being raped, people being murdered with witnesses all around. Yet no one intervenes; instead, they whip out their smartphone to record the violent crime. They walk by, just like the rabbi and sadducee in Jesus' parable about the Good Samaritan, refusing to help the injured man along the street. Illicit sex, adultery, sleeping with anyone and everyone has become commonplace in today's world. Quasi-pornographic scenes are in daytime television, even children's shows. Don't even get me started on football games or what is called musical performances in the 21st century.

Much of the church is addicted to porn. One person on social media (who claimed to be a Christian) didn't understand what was even wrong with watching porn. I had to shake my head and cringe at the blatant deception of the enemy. Pastors and men of the church are defiled by addictions to porn. Even women in the church are. Oftentimes, a person is sexually traumatized as a child, the lust, the confusion, the perversion sets in at an early age. Someone may even introduced porn to him before he's even twelve years old.

Now, mind you, all of this is hush-hush. We do not talk about such things inside the church. These things simply don't happen to church folk, you know. With that standard of operations, these broken, traumatized people grow up to be adults with sexual indiscretions, open doors in their lives to the demonic without identifying why or how to *make the bad man stop.*

Let me first break down why porn is evil, in case you aren't quite sure. Porn is part of the multi-billion-dollar human trafficking industry. Kiddie porn is another atrocious piece of the puzzle here. Human beings are demeaned, their souls, their hearts are destroyed and broken. There is nothing godly, good or holy about it. Jesus said if you look with lust at a person, it's the same as if you've had sex with that person. We are commanded in Exodus not to commit adultery. We've heard this taught and preached for centuries; yet many of us don't fully comprehend why this is such an important command.

Illicit, immoral, illegal sex is evil. It gives power to the demonic realm. Think about it. In ancient days, many of the pagan temples had temple prostitutes. Worshipers would visit the temple and have sex with one of the temple prostitutes as part of their ritual. It was to glorify that god or goddess.

Joan Hunter teaches about sexual covenants. Beyond soul ties, when you have sexual intercourse with a person, you establish a spiritual covenant with him or her. You spiritually connect with that person. You enter into a covenant with that person. Even fantasy encounters, such as pornography, cause ungodly sexual covenants to form. Matthew 5:28 talks about how just looking at a woman with lust means you've committed adultery with her in your heart. We are challenged by Paul to bring every thought captive to the mind of Christ. Let's start doing just that.

To renounce those covenants, pray:

Father, I went into an ungodly covenant with ______. I repent for that sin. Take it from me now and put it on the cross, never to be held against me again I renounce that covenant in Jesus' name. Anything bad that came in through that covenant, take it from me now, in Jesus' name. Thank You, Jesus.

Sometimes bad things happened to us when we were young, we were not willing participants. In those situations, you need to break the unwanted covenants and forgive the person who abused you. Pray this:

Father, I was forced into an ungodly covenant with ________. I forgive _________ for that sin. Take it from ______ now and put it on the cross, never to be held against _____ again. I renounce and break that covenant in Jesus' name. Anything bad that came in through that covenant, take it from me now in Jesus' name. I command the trauma, fear, shame and guilt of that experience to go, in Jesus' name. Thank you, Jesus.

(More on Joan's teachings about sexual covenants can be found in *Healing the Whole Man Handbook.*)

Jesus is coming back for a blameless, spotless Bride. A pure Ekklesia without spot or wrinkle. Let's continue with the cleansing, purging and pruning process to get us ready.

Now that we've addressed that, let's move onto thoughts and actions.

We have the ability to tell our own minds what to think. Father created us with the will to help you do things. It's like the engine of a car. You steer and press the gas pedal, the will gets it done. We need to start being intentional about what gets our attention, what we think.

Let's start with taking responsibility for our own thoughts, words and actions. No blaming someone else anymore for what you think, feel or do. No more excuses. No more blaming it on the trauma you've endured. Own every part of you, every broken, messed up piece of you. Recognize you have been hiding in shame from God because of sin, trauma, failures, abuse, mistreatment. Choose today to run to Him instead of hiding anymore. Your agreement, your own declarations shape your own life. Choose to reframe your problem by shifting the focus. Realize that God uses problems to increase your anointing, to expand your territory. Start looking for the places where your tent pegs are being moved rather than focusing on the problem. Look at what the Lord is doing in you and around you.

Satan tries to draw you away from the Secret Place, your seat in the Throne Room of God. The cares of this world, the deceitfulness of riches try to get your eyes off of God. When you head in the Lord's direction, the enemy tries to distract you. He wants to choke your faith out. We have to learn to trust God no matter what we see. We lose the battle when we quit trusting God. We are more than conquerors. It's time to act like it. Having faith means trusting what God says to be absolutely true.

Beloved, child, breathe Me in. I am at work. I am involved. Remain in Me as I am in you. Think higher thoughts. Take every thought captive as you focus on Me. Experience My peace, My rest in the midst of chaos. Your peace is from Me, not your situation or circumstance. It is not of this world. You can have My peace at any time, at all times. Worries and concerns dissipate in My Presence. Fear runs away in My Presence. Shame and guilt are unable to stand and must flee My presence. No unclean evil thing can be near My Presence. You are cleansed, renewed in My midst. Remain calm. You are in Me.

We ask Him for more, not realizing we will be required to withstand more, to bear the weight of more authority and responsibility when it comes. We will pay the price to carry more of the anointing. He tests us regularly to determine if we are ready to bear the weight of what He wants to give us. Just as you train with weights, slowly increasing your weights week by week as you build up stronger muscles, we build spiritual muscles as we train with Jesus. More and more weight gets added as we grow and strengthen our spiritual might.

It's time we realized we don't need to show up for every fight we see. David asked the Lord prior to battle if it was his fight. If the Lord was sending him in. We need to contend for the victories we've won and defend our territory. We need greater discernment and learn to focus on not letting the enemy get in godly relationships. We should learn his strategies and tactics (stepping into the war room and learning how he operates). Jesus said the enemy comes to steal, kill and destroy. He hates joy, love and peace. He is against family, community, union and unity, harmony. Therefore, he will plant seeds of discord, twisted communication, strife, division, rebellion, divorce, guilt, shame, jealousy, resentment, bitterness, criticism to get you spun up and angry for no good reason against your friend, family member or church member.

When an issue arises, when someone asks for prayer, brings her problems to you, seek the face of God in that moment. Ever read a post on social media that jerks your chain? Do you realize you can choose to walk away and/or keep scrolling? Not every battle is worth you losing your peace over. Discern which fight He has called you to enter and which ones are distractions sent by the enemy. Get strategic about when you use your weapons and arsenal.

You may have heard that anointing breaks the yoke. Jane Hamon teaches Shalom peace comes when you destroy the authority of chaos. If chaos has been reigning in your home and in your head, it's time to decree

Shalom into your life. Assign peace to be a sentinel over your mind, guarding you from chaos and strife.

Declare today, "I decree Shalom over my body, my mind, my heart. I decree Shalom over my house, my work, my family. Nothing missing, nothing lacking, nothing broken."

Are you ready to storm the gates?

I want an army that will storm the prisons, that will break down walls, that will infiltrate the enemy's kingdom to rescue My captured children. I want warriors who will worship Me and advance My Kingdom in everything they do. I want soldiers loyal to My Name who will enter battle without blinking an eye. Knowing they walk from victory to victory. I want soldiers who will use their skills, their talents, their strengths, to find My children who have been hidden in dungeons by the enemy. I want brave, fearless fierce men and women who abandon it all for the sake of the call. The call of My heart: to rescue my children. I want warriors who will go wherever I call them. Who storm the enemy's beaches, climb his prison walls, attack in My name. Who fear nothing on this earth. I want sons and daughters to arise who bear My heart to the nations. Who endure, who embrace suffering for My purpose, for My glory. I want worshipping warriors who will risk their lives to rescue their siblings. A special force that goes wherever I send them, ready to do whatever it takes to break the captives free.

Chapter Fifty-One

There Is a Sound

There is a sound only heard in the deepest of forests, in the heart of the jungle, the depths of the ocean, far out to sea.

There is a sound heard by seekers, by wayfarers, by those who follow the dove where He may lead, who chase the butterfly of transformational life wherever He may lead.

There is a sound only heard when you leave the known, the seen, the felt world and go after the unseen, the mysterious, the unknown. When you abandon it all for the sake of the call of your Lord and Savior.

There is a sound of majesty, of greatness, of love, of power that yearns to be heard by a people who want their inheritance, a people who know their identity as much-loved sons and daughters of the Most High King. The sound awaits those who are willing to pursue, to press in, to seek first the Kingdom of God and His Righteousness. The call is to surrender one's life on His altar and let Him lead wherever He wills. To relinquish control, to forgo understanding every situation, every circumstance, every plan and just follow the gentle Dove, to trust beyond what is known, what is seen and just go with God.

Will you pursue it? Will you go until you hear the *SOUND?*

There's a sound only found in the quietness of the soul. When you silence the distractions of the world, when you turn off all music, TV, close down every open app on your phone or mobile device. Stop storyboarding in your mind. Quit thinking about what ifs and wondering about your circumstances and just be still before your Lord. Silence everything else and just listen. Let the Father share His heart with you to reveal hidden sounds to you.

Sounds are being released that were silenced for centuries. They have never been heard by man before. My fiery ones are listening to My song and My studio, receiving new sounds for earth.

A tsunami is coming. A violent raging ocean, wave after wave roaring through the waters. A current so strong, mortal man cannot survive it. An unstoppable energy. A force that the earth has yet to experience. A quake so deep in the ocean's floor has fractured the pre-existing base of life. The resulting tsunami will flood the nations. No continent, no island, no country is safe from this coming barrage of waves. Every land, every tongue will experience this overwhelming, great, undoing of normal. This supernatural, this extraordinary movement of water, this energy force will flood the nations. Every land, forever changing the people, the setting, the environment, the ecosystems. This tsunami is the Living Water of Christ. This supernatural force is His body of believers flooding the world with His living water. It will change things forever.

We are the tsunami of Living Water, sent out to flood the world.

Chapter Fifty-Two

Take the Land

Go for it. Trust Him. He's giving you the desires of your heart. It's time to walk into new things, new adventures. No fear. Just go for it. Don't you know we've been given dominion over the land? Subdue the land, the terrestrial realm. Anything that manifests in the natural realm, you have dominion and authority over it. Subdue it.

You are carrying the burden of the land you have been given dominion over. You are NOT to identify with the burden of the land. Instead, you are to take dominion over it and subdue it. Flip the burden to its opposite. Don't agree with the problems, focus on the solutions.

Walking in the world's culture means you're in danger of forgetting who you are. Focusing on problems instead of solutions steals your hope and peace, destroys your joy. When you find yourself dwelling on the circumstances, the issues, the dilemmas, you will recognize what's happening. You will, with the Lord's help, shift gears and bring hope into the situation. You will learn to see His goodness and promises, focusing instead on what the Lord is doing and trusting He is faithful. No longer laboring in turmoil and torment, instead, you'll walk in the knowledge you have a good Father whose mercies are new every morning. It is time to be filled with the glory of God. pre-believers should be magnetized to you because you have something they need. Jesus. Kingdom attracts people who don't know the Lord. Be prepared. You'll repel the religious ones. Remember, the traditional religious people didn't like Jesus; He disrupted their traditions and rituals with Truth and Grace.

What is accepted, encouraged, tolerated in your house is what's passed down generation to generation. You've now entered a new season. What was standard procedure before, the normal benchmark of forward progress is no longer. I am your Provider. Be prepared to receive. Position yourself for blessings and favor. Goodness is coming to you. Abide in Me as you focus on Me.

Raise up inside your family to go into the world and advance the Kingdom. Teach them a new way. Previously, you relied on paychecks from your employers for your provision. Now you will see the goodness of God as I AM brings the harvest into the storehouses. I got you. Trust Me. I will not have My children begging for bread. Focus on your budget, your financial plan. Resources that have been promised and prophesied for years are being released from heaven now. Stand on the promises of God. You mind your saving and spending; I'll mind the income. A year from now will look drastically different than now. Be flexible and adaptive.

Chapter Fifty-Three

Come Alive

Come alive.

Oh dead one who lies in a grave, wrapped in burial cloths, comatose as still as death, One who was broken, shattered, pierced and crowned with thorns.

Come alive.

Crucified one. You were spit upon, tortured, whipped, scorn, beaten and abused.

Come alive. The gentle whisper of Holy Spirit floats into a borrowed grave.

Come alive. The words are spoken by a Spirit whose strength is unmatched.

"*Come alive,*" is shouted; it reverberates against the walls of the tomb.

A wounded Lamb arises from His grave.

A victorious Lion of Judah emerges from the tomb.

A risen Savior comes forth, with the keys to death and hell in His hands.

A war cry resounds from the mountain tops today. *COME ALIVE,* the Trinity cries out to the Bride of Christ. The Power that resurrected Jesus is within you. Come alive. Breathe in grace. Breathe in joy. Gasp as you grasp love, boundless love. Tremble as you feel the Resurrection Power course through your body, from the top of your head to the soles of your feet.

Come alive, beloved. You are a new creation, filled with new wine. Come alive and release His power on the earth.

The enemy has tried to keep you from understanding who you really are. To know what your calling and destiny are, to know what was written about you in the books of destiny in heaven. Stop trying to walk in someone else's destiny. Stop envying what they have, what they're doing, what they've accomplished. Focus on your own relationship with the Lord, ask Him directly for revelation on what He has in mind for you to accomplish in this life. Get to where you are fully relying on God for your next step, your next move. "God, if You don't show up, I'm done," is a challenge He loves to get.

Remove sin, iniquity, transgressions, generational curses from your lives. There are many resources available for support in doing this. I recommend Arthur Burk's teachings, Natasha Grbrich's *Repentance,* and John Sandford's books: *Transforming the Human Spirit and Healing the Wounded Spirit. The Adversary* by Mark Bubeck.

Recover the authority you and your ancestors gave up. Wherever sin is in your life, you have given authority over to the enemy. It is time to take the authority back and use it to advance the Kingdom of God everywhere you go.

Jesus said, "The enemy has nothing in common with me." Beloved, that is the key to healing and setting others free. We have to have nothing in common with the sin, the ailment, the curse. We come in the name of the Lord of Hosts and cut off the giant's head, so the witnesses know there is a God in Israel.

Only the Lord goes before you to your frontier. Beloved, there is a wilderness pathway calling you into uncharted waters, unmapped territories. This is where He is calling you to go, to explore, to seek for the treasure He has hidden there for you to discover. As you obey Him, as you go higher, deeper, farther, He will lead you to the hidden treasures. You cannot stay in the safe comfort zones anymore. You were never meant to abide there. You were not designed for hanging about in safe harbors. You have been called to deeper waters, higher mountains and wilder jungles.

Will you heed His call?

Chapter Fifty-Four

Who's Really Scared of Whom?

Where's your momentum taking you?

We were built for momentum, for moving, flowing, being in motion. The question is: Have we been moving forward or backward? Have we been advancing the Kingdom of God or in a retreat mode, continually giving ground to the forever loser (as Tim Sheets calls him)?

It's time to take territory back from the enemy and advance the kingdom. Beloved, ignore those no trespassing signs of the enemy and get after it. Jesus said the gates of hell would not prevail against His ekklesia. We have been living in expectation of being attacked, under siege, oppression for far too long.

Realizing the enemy is out to kill you, destroy you, steal your identity and destiny, when you use deductive reasoning, you figure out he is that scared of you walking out the call of God on your life. He is pulling out all the stops in order to keep you from reaching it.

This might be a complete shift from your religious mindsets about life on earth and spiritual warfare. It might be a challenge to what you've learned until now. Let me tell you a story to explain my point. Grab your cookies, milk and blanket and have a seat here on the floor next to me. It's storytime at the library.

Years ago, after leading mission trips and mission teams for several years, being the person in charge, I was going on a trip as a team member. I was not a team leader or in charge of the whole trip. I said I would be like Tigger from Winnie the Pooh and jumping around, spreading joy everywhere I went. I planned on being the floater, jumping in to help wherever I could, wherever was needed. We were putting new metal roofs on homes in a mountain village in Honduras.

There was no running water in this village. Guess what, no electricity either. We got there Sunday afternoon and by Monday morning I had a horrible toothache. Tylenol barely took the edge off the pain. We were out in the middle of the jungle, yes, we even saw a pandemonium of green parrots fly by one day. We were so high up in the mountains, we were near clouds. I was begging for painkillers from anyone who had a stash packed in their backpack. I took so much Advil and Tylenol in those four days, the mission pastor lectured me about the damage they could do to my kidneys and liver if I took too many. I didn't care; my tooth was in horrendous pain.

I had brain fog, couldn't remember basic Spanish, or the name of anyone i had just met in the village. I was cold and slept under two sleeping bags at night. I was exhausted, napping frequently throughout the day. I barely trekked outside of the school where we fixed coffee and meals.

The team prayed for my healing Tuesday night. The next day I woke up looking like Cindy Lou from Whoville on the Grinch. My face was swollen up like Elephant Man. Thursday night I stayed back at the school while the team went to a worship service on the mountain top at a house. I didn't feel well enough to go and hiking anywhere made my heart race, and I could then feel the heartbeat in my tooth. My team leader put a quick stop to that.

When I asked Papa what was going on, why was this happening, what was I to learn in the midst of this, an evil being as tall as the building I was in showed up. Reminded me of Golaith, taunting and trying to intimidate. I took one look at him and realized I was ill, not in any condition to fight, and alone, so I went running to Papa and jumped into His lap, asking Him to deal with the giant.

Next thing I remember, I looked around the room and the large being was gone. We came down off the mountain the next day. When I had a chance to chat with the local pastor, he informed me of the witchcraft and voodoo rituals that occur on the very mountain we were working on. The locals knew I had shown up as soon as I set foot there. He asked if I was a prophetic intercessor, which I confirmed. He then said I was the strongest prophetic one on my small team, which is why I had been targeted, why the enemy attempted to take me out. My intercessors back in the USA were having a hell week as well (most never would even tell me anything that happened, they just said it was an intense battle). One older woman had a back injury recur that hadn't happened in 30+ years. I seriously ticked them off just because I was on that mountain. The gospel of Jesus Christ had just been preached there for the first time within five years of me going there. It was still very dark, impoverished and oppressed area.

Upon returning to the States, I immediately went to the dentist. He looked accusatory at my husband after taking an x-ray of my mouth. He said the tooth was broken clean across at the gumline, just as if I had been punched in the face. He wanted to know what happened. Did a board fall off a roof and hit me in the face?

How do you explain to a dentist a supernatural being punched you in the face? "While I was sleeping, I got into a spiritual battle with a local strongman...."

When I talked to a close friend who is apostolic, without missing a beat, she asked a simple question. "Were you walking in your identity as a child of God, ruling and reigning from your seat in heavenly places as soon as you landed there?"

"I wasn't leading. I wasn't in charge. I was just a team member. I didn't have to lead...."

"But you still have to walk in the knowledge of who you are and the authority you carry, the power within you. Anywhere you go, you are still you."

"Oh crap. Oh no." It dawned on me exactly what had happened. I was so focused on not leading and being in charge, being along for the ride, I failed to remember my true identity. I wasn't embracing my identity. The identity that says I am a much-loved daughter of the Most High King, called to change the world and set the captives free.

Now, beloved, do you see the importance of knowing who you are, whose you are and your calling? Do you grasp how important it is to step into the high calling glory of God? To embrace your identity and walk in it, covered in His grace and goodness.

I'll never know how differently that week would have gone if I had shown up as the much-loved child of God, fully confident in her position. If my eyes were open spiritually then, what would I have seen on the mountaintop?

Chapter Fifty-Five

When the Glory Fire Comes

Your fire is a furnace that never sleeps. (Look up Martin Smith ~ The Fire Never Sleeps and check out the lyrics.) Therefore, abiding in Your Presence is remaining in the fire. Impurities burn off. The hotter the fire, the more purifying that's occurring.

We need to put on flame-guarded attire, able to withstand the fiery arrows of the enemy because it was forged and adorned in the fires of His glory. Every root of every weed in the garden of our souls is burnt away in the depths of His Fire. We are cleansed, renewed, restored, redeemed, and rested. We are consumed by Your blazing fire.

Drawing close to You means drawing near the blazing furnace of Your glory. All else melts away in Your Presence. Nothing can withstand it.

Come, Lord, set fire to us. Burn away anything that's not of You.

Come, Lord Jesus, come.

I am about to break out.

I am about to break loose.

I am about to break free of the religious bindings, the traditional boxes, and the ritualistic standards man has put upon Me.

I will no longer be kept inside a box.

I am pouring out My Glory upon the nations, the city streets, the schools, the prisons, the city halls, the offices, the malls, even the bars will feel the weight of My glory, the glory of My goodness. I am about to flood the land with My glory. Wells of revival shall bubble up once again for the greatest harvest of all. I have heard the cries of My people. I have heard their travailing, their pleas for help. I will answer them by awakening My church. As they rend their hearts for change, humbled and desperate, I will rend the heavens and pour out an anointing, a move of God the world has never seen before. All of heaven waits with bated breath for this kairos moment.

My glory pours out as the wells spring up, the rains fall.

Revival is breaking out in the streets. Supernatural signs and wonders shall occur everywhere. On city streets, country roads, highways and byways. I will not be denied. I am the Breaker. Fences, barricades, walls, moats, whatever man with the dark one's help has erected physically or mentally, emotionally or spiritually to keep ME out cannot withstand the full-on assault of My love. Nothing can withstand the battering ram of My goodness and mercy. Towers, museums, palaces, temples, skyscrapers, anything built on the shifting sand of the world, the enemy's kingdom shall crumble into the sea as My glory falls upon the earth.

Let faith arise.

As you set your hope on Me, I manifest blessings beyond measure in you and for you. As you seek Me, I pursue you in greater measure. Child, do you not realize I won't stop until I have ALL of you?

You, beloved, are a revival fire. Everywhere you go, you light up your world. Shine in the grocery store. Illuminate the school, the city streets, the town hall with My love. Declare My promises in every moment, every situation. You are My hands and feet. I have filled you with My glory. Let it flow out unto the world around you. You are a wellspring of glory fire. It's time to release it to the world.

Do not fear when you see the failure of certain buildings, banks, businesses. Just as the Titanic sank, man-made monumental things shall fall and crumble into the sea. I am allowing those things to crash to open My children's eyes to see Truth. I am removing the idols from their lives by crushing them. As they see their false gods fall before their eyes, they realize I am the only God. I will use this to open their eyes to who I am.

They ask for My glory to fall.

They seek My face.

They want My presence.

Then when it falls, when I show up, they stand still, lie still, sit still. Or one of them speaks to the rest for an hour or so.

My glory carries My grace with it. My grace to move mountains, to shake the earth, to shift atmospheres, to manifest breakthrough, to heal the sick, to liberate the captives, open blind eyes. I am pouring out my glory upon the earth and My people must learn to walk in it, to move in it, to work in it. TO find out what I desire for them to do with My strength in that moment.

It's time for suddenlies to take place. Instantaneous healings, creative miracles, supernatural weight loss, and more.

My children must be ready to carry the glory fire, to burn with abandon as they feel My heat intensify. Anything not of Me has been burnt off and now Love erupts wherever they go. They move when I say move. They stop when I say stop. They go where I go. They do as I do.

Chapter Fifty-Six

New Base Camp

The pure in heart shall see God. We have heard this verse for decades. Yet, in another verse the Word talks about how wicked man's heart is. If man's heart is wicked, then how in the world can we become pure in heart?

We start with worship, with praise. With focusing solely on the Godhead. Ultimate intimacy with the Father purifies us. Contend for His glory to manifest. Let everything else go. What you thought was your ministry. Your expectations. Let Him take you higher. There is no more striving. The King is looking for worshippers who worship in spirit and truth.

Let go of all that has entangled and ensnared you. Be caught up in His glory being released upon the earth. Draw near to Him. Run after Him. He promises to let you catch Him.

Being pure in heart requires a change to our base camp, our default position.

Build a New Base Camp

What is your default mode? When life happens, where do you land? Where is the crash point? We all fall back to base camp when things get hectic, when they get stressful.

If you were to climb Mount Everest, you would notice there are two base camps. In order to reach the summit, you must stop returning to Base Camp 1 and instead, press on toward Base Camp 2. When you climb higher on the Glory Mountain of Faith, you can no longer retreat to the first base camp. You need to continue on until you reach the next one, and then the next one, and the one after that.

As you transform into His likeness and grow stronger in faith, you'll discover your default mode changes as times goes by. As you renew your mind in Christ, new neural pathways are plowed in your brain. You think new thoughts and talk a new language, the language of Heaven. You will find evidence of transformation as you notice that you no longer downshift to a Negative Nancy, Groucho Marx or Grumpy Dwarf.

You learn to cooperate with Him, instead of resist Him.

We ask Him for more, not realizing we will be required to withstand more, to bear the weight of more authority and responsibility when it comes. We will pay the price to carry more of the anointing. He tests us regularly to determine if we are ready to bear the weight of what He wants to give us. Just as you train with weights, slowly increasing your weights week by week as you build up stronger muscles, we build spiritual muscles as we train with Jesus.

What does bearing more weight look like in the natural? How do we see this play out in our own lives?

Glad you asked. Grab the milk and cookies. It's story time.

"If you hire one more woman over the age of fifty, I'm going to smack you alongside the head," I sniped at my CEO years ago. See, he'd hired four of them over the previous year or two. Each one had targeted me, sabotaged my career, tried to steal my clients ... you get the idea. A pair of them took me to lunch one day, silly me thought we were going to have a nice time together. They pounced like wild cats once out of the office and the earshot of anyone else. They informed me, "If it were up to me, I'd fire you right now." On and on the conversation went.

Mind you, I was in the midst of setting up a partnership with a Fortune 50 company to sell our product to our target market. They wanted to take over the account and get rid of me. The CEO and CFO both knew what was going on.

I finally found another job (they contacted me to come in for an interview) and gratefully left that company. *And then,* years later, Holy Spirit and I were doing some deep uprooting and healing. I was surrendering anything and everything impeding me from drawing closer to Him, being filled with glory. Chasing after more of Yahweh. The Lord brought these women to mind and told me I needed to forgive, to tear out the bitter roots of resentment in my heart. I needed to let go of bitter expectations and bitter judgments against older women. They weren't all going to attack. They weren't all going to be jealous and judgmental toward me.

I had to realize my own bitter roots were causing me to see others through a skewed lens and attracting the same actions and behavior. These bitter roots limited bonding with older women and finding mentors for me.

A moment of raw truth: it took *multiple* times of renouncing bitterness, forgiving them, letting go of the right to be angry and upset, speaking blessing over them instead before I felt a true shift. Honestly, it's like a Texas Thistle. Those suckers come back with just a sliver of root left in the ground that you missed. Holy Spirit is actually nudging me now to do another round of repentance and blessing for this situation. Layers and onions, I tell ya, layers and onions.

Chapter Fifty-Seven

Crisis of Faith

When you head in the Lord's direction, the enemy tries to distract you. He tries to draw you away from the Secret Place, your seat in the Throne Room of God. The cares of this world, the deceitfulness of riches, physical ailments, family drama, work situations are all different things he'll try to use to get you out of your seat with Jesus. He will use anything he can to come after you. He knows where the toeholds are, the open doors, the weak points in your armor. He already knows your Achilles heel, your battle injury that hasn't quite healed fully yet. He knows where to strategically hit you to get the effect he wants.

He wants to choke your faith out.

Ever had a crisis of faith related to finances, to healing? What do I mean by a crisis of faith? Allow me to explain.

In 2019, we had heard the Lord calling us to leave the Mid-Atlantic region and move to Hill Country Texas. We had been preparing for the big move for months, packing up the house and barn, saying goodbye and so long to family and friends, finding a new place to live in Kerr County, finding a new church, and hopefully a job for me.

In May 2019, Rob and I visited Kerrville again, house searching and job searching. I interviewed with two companies and was agreeable to either position. It was a race in my mind to see which one panned out first. We found a fixer upper we thought had an amazing opportunity for growth and put an offer on it before heading back to Maryland.

A month later, we were booking Uhaul trailers, trucks and lining up drivers to assist with the long cross-country drive. I still hadn't received an official job offer yet, but we were moving forward with the plan set before us. I had told my boss what was going on and she advised me to wait until I had an official offer in hand before quitting. Then, as we approached Moving Day, she got antsy and wanted to know dates so she could plan accordingly with hiring replacements. As if I needed more stress about the whole situation at that point. I finally had to tell Papa, I trusted Him. I would obey His commands, follow His voice and let Him handle the details. They say the devil is in the details so I figured it was best for Papa to handle those.

On the Tuesday of the week we moved, I received the official job offer from the company in San Antonio and I immediately submitted my letter of resignation. I was giving two weeks' notice, with vacation time for the second week. Company policy said I had to be in town for the final work day so they changed my departure date to that Friday. No time for goodbye parties or a big hoorah. I was glad to get out of there anyways.

Sidebar: I negotiated for a pay increase so the offer wasn't even finalized until after we had moved to Texas.

He's always on time, but sometimes He likes to make us sweat a little about whether He's going to come through or not.

As I go back through journal entries from that period of my life, it's quite entertaining now to see how I continually brought my fears, concerns, stresses to the Lord. Every single time, He just gently pulled the lamb into His arms and held me close, "I got you, child. Just trust Me." Now I can reflect on those days and find it fun and exciting to think about how it was a tight-rope walk, where we had to rely on Him every day. I can encourage others in their own faith crises, to simply lean on Jesus. He's got this.

We have to learn to trust God no matter what we see. I didn't see how we'd pay two mortgage payments each month until I had a job in Texas. Our new mortgage loan wouldn't be approved without a job in Texas for me. Our house in Maryland didn't have any bites, any offers, any takers yet. In the midst of all of that, we made the choice to continue to trust and obey the Lord.

We lose the battle when we quit trusting God. When we choose to trust in man, in ourselves, in what we can see instead of holding on to faith. As Apostle Paul said, we are more than conquerors. It's time to act like it. Having faith means trusting what God says to be absolutely true. God said it. I believe it. That settles it.

But sometimes we're being enticed into battles that aren't really ours to fight. Sometimes the enemy is trying to distract us from our God-given purpose, from a frontline he knows he can't defend for very long. Keep reading to learn more.

Chapter Fifty-Eight

Is This My Fight?

Did you know you don't have to enter the battlefield for every fight you're invited to? Do you realize sometimes the enemy is trying to pick a fight with you and Papa is telling you to cease and desist? He's asking you to lie down your sword and step into His arms instead. You're called to abide in His peace in the midst of chaos and confusion, grief and shame, not begin boxing with shadows.

It's time we realized we don't need to show up for every fight we see. David asked the Lord prior to battle if it was his fight. If the Lord was sending him in. Check out 1 Samuel 23 and 30 for just a few examples. David, the king who was a man after God's own heart, knew enough to consult the Lord before rushing into war. Shouldn't we exercise the same wisdom ourselves?

I have seen requests for intercession, for prayer online before. I have felt compassion on the person in need and opened up my messages in preparation to send them a heartfelt prayer, to approach the King on their behalf. As I begin to type a message, I am halted. My steps are arrested and I hear a "No" in my spirit. "This is not your fight, dear one." The person in question wasn't a close friend or family member. I simply wanted to help.

I have learned over the last few years, intercession means standing in the gap. Literally, you are standing before the judge, the king, the Lord on behalf of this person asking for solutions, provisions, healing. You are covering for that person. Are you ready to deal with whatever comes your way, from that person? Do you have the authority, the permission, the metron to do so?

Allow me to explain. Moms have special authority when praying for their children. To be clear, I'm still unpacking this revelation and don't pretend to fully grasp it yet. But what I know, when a mama hits her knees and is crying out for God to move on her child's behalf, I don't care if that baby is six months old or sixty years old, God hears the mama hanging onto the altar, crying and pleading for Jesus to save her baby.

Case in point, I was home recently to spend quality time with my parents. The first night there I was battling horrible tooth pain, refer to the giant in Honduras story for background on this tooth saga, and I was asking the Lord to fill my mouth with glory fire, to flush it with fire.

The next morning my friend Stephanie came to visit and, of course, the tooth came up in conversation. Mind you, this is the same friend who quizzed me on walking in my identity in Honduras afterwards. I mentioned the battle the night before and my mom piped up. She'd been pretty quiet in the conversation until that point. She explained how she felt I was under attack during the night and simply prayed for me. No idea what was going on, battling congestive heart failure and her own health issues, but when her baby girl was in need, she picked up her sword and started swinging.

Fathers also have authority in this way. They call forth identity and blessing, providing a covering for the entire household. They have a separate and important responsibility for praying over their families. But back to mothers.

Mom has authority and power to intervene because she gave birth to me. My husband has authority and power as well. I've learned sometimes pain will subside with a simple laying on of hands and short prayer by him. I can pray and pray and pray under my breath and then, finally, ask for help. That's when things change in a moment.

Full transparency moment: eons ago, we were in marital counseling, and I was angry with him. I didn't want to sit near him or touch him. We were in a battle for our marriage at the time and I ended up with the only migraine I've ever had while in session. (Watch how Jehovah Sneaky intervenes.) The only way the pain would subside was for me to lay on the couch with my head in my husband's lap. Remember how I was mad at him and didn't want to sit near him, let alone touch him. But God didn't care about my own rebellious and ornery attitude at that moment. He knew what would bring healing and restoration.

But sometimes the Lord says no. When our fleshly self wants to help, wants to build a bathroom for everyone as a missionary friend in a developing country once said, and we don't think about assignment, calling, purpose. Does this align with that? David asked if the Lord was sending him into battle, wanting to know if it was a distraction from his assignment or part of his assignment. He was focused on the Lord, serving and praising Him, not just flitting around from flower to tree blossom like a butterfly. Like many of us do.

Let's learn to abide in His presence and ask what would you have me do or say today.

Chapter Fifty-Nine

Contend for the Battleground

Don't lose the victory by not contending for your win.

We need to defend the territory we've taken. We should stop letting the enemy take back the territory we just won back from him. It's time to learn to contend for the land. You started spending your mornings with coffee and Jesus. Whether it's five minutes or fifty minutes, it's a focused time with the Lord. Don't let distractions dissuade you from your commitment to spend that time each day. You've been faithfully speaking blessing over your children every day, don't stop. Don't let their actions and behavior steal that from you. Address the behavior but speak *LIFE* over them ... when they can hear it.

We need greater discernment and to focus on not letting the enemy get in godly relationships. It is time to learn to know his strategies and tactics, to step into the war room and learn how he operates. Jesus said the enemy comes to steal, kill, and destroy. Worm hates joy, love, and peace. He is against family, community, union and unity, harmony. Therefore, he will plant seeds of discord, twisted communication, strife, division, rebellion, divorce, guilt, shame, jealousy, resentment, bitterness, criticism to get you spun up and angry for no good reason against your friend, family member or church member. Recognize his tactics and respond accordingly. Flip it to the opposite spirit.

I once was at a prophetic conference with a friend and we were grabbing breakfast at the hotel before the event started. We were giggling like school girls, full of the joy of the Lord. Well, you know *that's* going to trigger the religious spirits. Suddenly, there's a guy who worked at the hotel joining our conversation. He immediately brought up the age-old debate question of "Why does a good God let bad things happen to good people?" Off to the races we went, to a theological debate. Strife, sadness, bitterness, resentment, confusion had entered the conversation. As BB King sang, "The thrill is gone."

I realized what was happening as my little evangelist friend wanted to keep trying to share the love of Jesus with this man. I explained graciously we had to leave and make our way to the conference before we were late. Then Miss Evangelist eagerly told the man we'd be back the next morning for breakfast and could continue the conversation then. Honestly, I could have smacked her for saying that. I knew he was operating in a joy-stealing spirit and not interested in a real conversation about the goodness of God and building community. Talk about casting pearls before swine!

Chapter Sixty

Glory Wildfires

Drops of fire rain are falling all across the land. Glory fires are being set in every region, every nation. Glory rain falls and the embers land upon the dry, empty stalks of discord, disorder, disappointment. The straw-like weeds of depression, fear, anxiety and confusion ignite and are consumed by the glory fire. Anything and everything that's not the Kingdom of Heaven will be burnt up by this raging fire.

Just as wildfires rage across the arid lands untethered and uncontrolled, this fire will rage throughout the homes, schools, city halls, county courthouse, churches and capitals. No one is safe from this fire. No one can hide. No one can escape the tsunami of fire spreading across the land.

Are you ready for the consuming fire of God to rage through your community, your work, your family, your home, yourself? The embers of His fire are being fanned into flames and are spreading across the land. The fire is cleansing and purifying, bringing forth the pure gold and silver. Allowing sanctified ones to arise who are solely focused on glorifying Him and not seeking the glory for themselves.

Amidst this raging fire, He is burning up oppressive patriarchal ways. Humankind has oppressed the female gender of the species for centuries. The enemy has strategized and executed plans for millennia to keep women in poverty, in slavery, in confusion and covered with a blanket of lies. Eve's daughters have been under a banner of self-loathing, self-rejection, mistaken identity, overrun by lust, lies and a legacy of detrimental diatribes. The enemy does not want Eve's daughters to discover their true identities. He has fought tooth and nail for ages to ensure they were kept in captivity. Princesses hidden in towers, hidden in cottages, working their fingers to the bone. Never loved, never treasured, never adored and adorned.

Suddenly, a Prince of Peace arrives on the scene. This Lion of Judah charges into the darkest areas, the deepest pits, the highest towers, the deepest oceans. He rescues His bride, His Father's daughters from captivity, from slavery. He heals the brokenhearted, comforts those who mourn. He gives beauty for ashes, strength for fear, gladness for mourning, peace for despair. He erases every lie the enemy told. He breaks every chain holding her down. He burns off every rope that ties her fast. He rips off every helmet of untruth, hatred, and mistaken identity. Every weapon ever used against her is thwarted. Every wound is healed.

He takes each one into His arms, whispering their names as He calls forth their destinies. He proclaims them as His beloved. His beautiful bride. They are beautiful jewels in His crown. They are called to so much more than they ever imagined. They are the Father's image. They are the world's mother, the nurturer, the comforter, the calming voice to a hurting child, the nurse who tends the sick with a compassionate heart. The Daughters of Yahweh who carry anointing oil to heal the sick, to rescue their sisters and brothers. They are the worshipers, the dancers who pour out their alabaster boxes unto the Lord. Women have a special place in Papa's heart. Daddy's girls. Beauty, brains, gentleness, mercy, kindness, peacemakers.

Papa has a message for His sons and His daughters:

My Son came to earth to give you back your authority. He restored the authority Adam had given away in the garden. When you accept Jesus as Lord and Savior, as you renounce the earth as your home and choose to be seated in heavenly places with Me instead, you receive power and authority as a son of God, as a daughter of the Most High King. Beloved, you have barely scratched the surface of the authority you carry as My child. You bring heaven to earth. You give the world glimpses of what heaven looks like when you move with Me. Freedom. Joy. Peace. Love. Grace. Goodness. Order. Honor. Respect. Humility. Compassion.

When you exert your authority in your mind, your body, your soul, you advance My Kingdom. As you step out in faith and into the authority, I have reserved for you, you move into your destiny. As you relinquish burdens, iniquities, unforgiveness, pain, trauma, I trade each of those for something else.

Chapter Sixty-One

Come to the Water

> The anatomy of a good fight is perception, mindset, and language all lined up with sovereignty and majesty. ~ Graham Cooke

It is time for us to learn to see obstacles to overcome as accelerants to growth. Instead of resenting the blockage, begrudging the problem, be excited about what Papa has in store. For every problem, He has provisions already lined up. He has a particular aspect of Himself (Provider, Healer, Redeemer, Friend, Comforter, etc.) He wants you to discover in the midst of this situation. He has a plan for you in the process, this journey. He sees you in the future and He sees a reformed, renewed, revived you who persevered and pushed through to the other side.

There is a Voice crying out to the world, "Come to the water all who are thirsty. Come to the table all who are hungry."

Yet all over the world there are thirsty children, desperate for a glass of water. Safe water to drink, not contaminated with toxins, parasites and feces.

All over the world, there are children who are hungry, starving to death day by day because they have nothing to eat.

Who will take them food and water? Who will go?

All over the world people try to fill their stomachs, their hearts, their souls with anything and everything but God's love. They desperately search for something to satisfy that craving within them for more, for connection, for knowledge life is worth living, for a love that never fails. They try to fit every puzzle piece into the hole they have inside but it is never the right piece. The Father's love is the only piece that fits the spot.

Who will take His love to them? Who will go?

Years ago, I read *Your God Is Too Safe* by Mark Buchanan. This passage from his book nails the commissioning we have received.

> As the Father has sent Me, I am sending you ... a call into the world, in all its broken and heartbreaking beauty, in all its seediness and neediness, to be a Christlike presence. We go in the same authority, with the same power, with the same heart after God. It means we walk by the Spirit and become like Jesus from the inside out.

In the process of learning to walk by the Spirit, as we are transformed into the likeness of Christ, we find ourselves being stripped, purified, pruned and purged of anything and everything that's not of Him. As Mark put it, "God sometimes strips us in order to betroth us. He would sooner chase us with typhoons and leviathans into the holy wild than leave us marooned on borderland." We were born to be giant slayers. We were created and designed to rule with authority and power upon the earth. We were made in His image and we are charged with taking the kingdoms for the King. Are you willing to accept the charge?

Chapter Sixty-Two

The Bride Arrives

The King arises from His throne. The Prince of Peace stands as well. All of the witnesses and elders around the Room are standing, watching.

The giant doors swing open.

Trumpets blaring.

A melody spreads across the clouds as the Lover begins to sing,

You, My beloved, have finally come. My Bride, My darling has arrived. Your beauty takes My breath away. Your grace is felt all around you. Your power makes the enemy tremble. Your joy is tangible. Your love tears down walls. Your peace shifts atmospheres. Your commitment to be faithful until the end pulls Me in. One look of your eyes and I'm captured, breathless at your love and beauty. You are My long-awaited Bride.

Acknowledgments

To my beta readers: Niamh Jackson, Lindsay Hauser, Lisa Carpenter, Christy Mossberg, Nick Poe, Maggie Spangler, thank you for your encouragement and feedback.

To Wendy Hibbard and the Writing Room: thank you for sparking the writer within back in 2020.

Appendix

I Am Statements

Who You Are in Christ

1. I can do all things through Christ Jesus (Philippians 4:13).

2. I am submitted to God, and the devil flees from me because I resist him in the Name of Jesus (James 4:7).

3. I am complete in Him Who is the Head of all principality and power (Colossians 2:10).

4. I can quench all the fiery darts of the wicked one with my shield of faith (Ephesians 6:16).

5. I am alive with Christ (Ephesians 2:5).

6. I am free from the law of sin and death (Romans 8:2).

7. I am far from oppression, and fear does not come near me (Isaiah 54:14).

8. I am born of God, and the evil one does not touch me (1 John 5:18).

9. I am holy and without blame before Him in love (Ephesians 1:4; 1 Peter 1:16).

10. I have the mind of Christ (1 Corinthians 2:16; Philippians 2:5).

11. I am a doer of the Word and blessed in my actions (James 1:22,25).

12. I am a joint-heir with Christ (Romans 8:17).

13. I am more than a conqueror through Him Who loves me (Romans 8:37).

14. I am an overcomer by the blood of the Lamb and the word of my testimony (Revelation 12:11).

15. I am a partaker of His divine nature (2 Peter 1:3-4).

16. I am an ambassador for Christ (2 Corinthians 5:20).

17. I am part of a chosen generation, a royal priesthood, a holy nation, a purchased people (1 Peter 2:9).

18. I am the righteousness of God in Jesus Christ (2 Corinthians 5:21).

19. I am the temple of the Holy Spirit; I am not my own (1 Corinthians 6:19).

20. I am the head and not the tail; I am above only and not beneath (Deuteronomy 28:13).

21. I am the light of the world (Matthew 5:14).

22. I have the peace of God that passes all understanding (Philippians 4:7).

23. I have the Greater One living in me; greater is He Who is in me than he who is in the world (1 John 4:4).

24. I have received the gift of righteousness and reign as a king in life by Jesus Christ (Romans 5:17).

25. I have received the spirit of wisdom and revelation in the knowledge of Jesus, the eyes of my understanding being enlightened (Ephesians 1:17-18).

26. I have received the power of the Holy Spirit to lay hands on the sick and see them recover, to cast out demons, to speak with new tongues.

I have power over all the power of the enemy, and nothing shall by any means harm me (Mark 16:17-18; Luke 10:17-19).

27. I have put off the old man and have put on the new man, which is renewed in the knowledge after the image of Him Who created me (Colossians 3:9-10).

28. Give generously and generous gifts will be given back to you, shaken down to make room for more. Abundant gifts will pour out upon you with such an overflowing measure that it will run over the top! Your measurement of generosity becomes the measurement of your return." (Luke 6:38).

29. I have no lack for my God supplies all of my need according to His riches in glory by Christ Jesus (Philippians 4:19).

30. I show forth the praises of God Who has called me out of darkness into His marvel- ous light (1 Peter 2:9).

31. I am God's child for I am born again of the incorruptible seed of the Word of God, which lives and abides forever (1 Peter 1:23).

32. I am God's workmanship, created in Christ unto good works (Ephesians 2:10).

33. I am a new creature in Christ (2 Corinthians 5:17).

34. I am a spirit being alive to God (Romans 6:11;1 Thessalonians 5:23).

35. I am a believer, and the light of the Gospel shines in my mind (2 Corinthians 4:4).

36. I am His elect, full of mercy, kindness, humility, and longsuffering (Romans 8:33; Colossians 3:12).

37. I am forgiven of all my sins and washed in the Blood (Ephesians 1:7).

38. I am delivered from the power of darkness and translated into God's kingdom (Colossians 1:13).

39. I am redeemed from the curse of sin, sickness, and poverty (Deuteronomy 28:15- 68; Galatians 3:13).

40. I am firmly rooted, built up, established in my faith and over flowing with gratitude (Colossians 2:7).

41. I am called of God to be the voice of His praise (Psalm 66:8; 2 Timothy 1:9).

42. I am healed by the stripes of Jesus (Isaiah 53:5; 1 Peter 2:24).

43. I am raised up with Christ and seated in heavenly places (Ephesians 2:6; Colossians 2:12).

44. I am greatly loved by God (Romans 1:7; Ephesians 2:4; Colossians 3:12; 1 Thessalonians 1:4).

45. I am strengthened with all might according to His glorious power (Colossians 1:11).

46. I press on toward the goal to win the prize to which God in Christ Jesus is calling us upward (Philippians 3:14).

47. For God has not given us a spirit of fear; but of power, love, and a sound mind (2 Timothy 1:7).

48. My old identity has been co-crucified with Messiah and no longer lives; for the nails of his cross crucified me with him. And now the essence of this new life is no longer mine, for the Anointed One lives his life through me— we live in union as one! My new life is empowered by the faith of the Son of God who loves me so much that he gave himself for me, and dispenses his life into mine! (Galatians 2:20).

Prayers

Here are several prayers for self-reflection, opening your heart and soul for the Holy Spirit to move brings light and life into your being. These are guidelines to prompt your own healing journey and recovering lost territory.

Repent of Idolatry

Father God, I have put other gods before you. I have idolized (fill in the blank) (examples are celebrities, sports, my job, my family, my school, my children, my life, my house, my vehicle, my friends, my church, etc.) I put their needs and wants, their activities before spending time with You, before obeying Your Voice. I repent of these sins, Lord, and ask that you nail them to the cross. Never to be held against me again. Wash me clean in the blood of the Lamb. Apply anointing oil to every place where this iniquity has rooted into my system. Cleanse me with your Living Water, Lord. Thank you, Jesus.

Self-Protection Strongholds/Forgiving Others

Soften my heart, O Lord. Take this heart of stone and replace it with a heart of flesh. Tear down these walls I have erected to guard my heart, to protect myself. Destroy these walls I built to isolate myself from those who might love me or harm me. Bust through these walls my ancestors constructed eons ago. Walls that were to preserve self. Walls of shame, pride, fear, worry, despair, grief, guilt. Tear them down, Lord. I want to be truly free and fully Yours, heart, mind, body, soul and strength. Come, Immanuel, bring forth a new heart inside of me, one like Yours.

Lord, I give you permission to tear down any stronghold, any wall, any fortress I have built or allowed in my heart, soul or mind to protect myself, to prevent intimacy with You and others for fear of trauma, pain and betrayal. Kick down the walls. Shatter the glass ceilings. Remove any stronghold, eradicate anything in me that doesn't serve You, bring You Glory.

I forgive my mother, my father, my brother, my uncles and aunts, for not protecting me, saving me, loving me as I wanted to be loved. I forgive them for emotional, physical, mental abuse. I renounce agreement with the generational curse of melancholy, of sexual oppression, of confusion and chaos, of not being noticed or seen, of having bitter root judgments and expectations, of holding grudges, of self hatred and self rejection,

I break off all witchcraft and curses now in Jesus name.

I declare I have the Mind of Christ. I am loved and adored. I am accepted just as I am. I am safe in the Father's arms. Any structure in my realm that doesn't serve you, Jesus, tear it down.

Weight Loss

I renounce the lie that being chubby makes me unattractive, and will prevent unwanted sexual advances. I renounce the lie that my appearance has anything to do with being preyed upon by mankind and the demonic realm. I renounce the lie that the abuse, the rape, the molestation, the trauma was my fault, that I asked for it, that is was my fault. I come out of agreement with these lies right now in Jesus name.

I declare that I am being cleansed by the blood of the Lamb and washed clean with the Living Water.

Jesus, I give You, my broken and bleeding heart. I trust you and love you. I give You my heart to heal, to restore, to renew. Heal me, Lord, revive me and redeem me into the daughter of the King you created me to be.

Orphan's Heart

Lord, when I thought I was lost, forgotten and abandoned, You were there. When things seemed darkest, when I couldn't hear Your voice anymore, when I sought acceptance and attention from the wrong people, You were there all along. I give you my orphan heart, my fear of lack, my poverty mentality and replace it with the heart of a much-loved son, a knowledge of abundance and a life-giving mentality.